Library of Pastoral Care

THE PASTORAL CARE OF
THE BEREAVED

D1514877

The Library of Pastoral Care

TITLES ALREADY PUBLISHED

Sick Call: A Book on the Pastoral Care of the Physically Ill
Kenneth Child

Caring for the Elderly
H. P. Steer

The Pastoral Care of the Dying
Norman Autton

The Pastoral Care of the Bereaved
Norman Autton

IN PREPARATION

Casework and Pastoral Care
Jean Heywood

Preparing Couples for Marriage
Martin Parsons

The Principles and Practice of Pastoral Care
R. S. Lee

The Pastoral Care of the Emotionally Distressed
Chad Varah

Marriage Guidance
Kenneth Preston

Other volumes are planned

The
Pastoral Care of
The Bereaved

NORMAN AUTTON

Chaplain, St George's Hospital, London

LONDON
S·P·C·K
1967

First published in 1967
by S.P.C.K.
Holy Trinity Church
Marylebone Road
London N.W.1

Made and printed in Great Britain by
William Clowes and Sons, Limited
London and Beccles

TO ALL who mourn the loss of a loved one, that

COURAGE may be granted them to face the
emptiness of the days ahead;

COMFORT given them through the sympathy
and care of others;

STRENGTH offered them in the knowledge
of the love of Christ;

SURE AND CERTAIN HOPE found in
the Communion of Saints, and

REUNION assured for them hereafter.

Contents

Acknowledgements

Thanks are due to the following for permission to quote from copyright sources:

Abingdon Press: *Understanding Grief*, by Edgar N. Jackson.

American Psychiatric Association: "Symptomatology and Management of Acute Grief", by Erich Lindemann, in *The American Journal of Psychiatry* (Vol. 101, No. 2).

Dr Felix Brown and *The British Journal of Psychiatry* (Vol. 107): "Depression and Childhood Bereavement", by Felix Brown.

Cornish Brothers: *The Lamp still Burns*, by Marjorie Crosby.

Cresset Press: *Upon this Rock*, by Emile Cammaerts.

Cruse Clubs: *The Widow's Child*, by Margaret Torrie.

J. M. Dent & Sons, Ltd and E. P. Dutton Co.: *Selected Letters: 1896–1924* of Baron Friedrich von Hügel, edited by Bernard Holland.

Faber & Faber Ltd and The Seabury Press: *A Grief Observed*, by C. S. Lewis.

Faith Press: *Darkness no Darkness*, by Raymond Raynes, C.R.

Sigmund Freud Copyrights Ltd, Mr James Strachey, and The Hogarth Press to quote from *Mourning and Melancholia* in Volume XIV (1914–1916) of the Standard Edition of the *Complete Psychological Works of Sigmund Freud*.

Harper & Row, Inc.: *The Gessell Institute Book of Child Behaviour*, by Frances L. Ilg and Louise Bates Ames.

Harvard University Press: *Tusculan Disputations*, and *Letters to his Friends*, by Cicero; *Moralia*, by Plutarch; *Ad Lucilium Epistulae Morales*, by Seneca; *Letters*, by St Basil; *Select Letters*, by St Jerome; *De Mortalitate*, by St Cyprian; *On the Decease of Satyrus*, by St Ambrose.

The Holy Cross Press: *Spiritual Letters of Father Hughson,* o.h.c.

Longmans Green & Co. Ltd: *Personal Religion and the Life of Devotion,* by W. R. Inge.

Methuen & Co. Ltd and Harper & Row, Inc.: *The Life of Oscar Wilde,* by Hesketh Pearson.

The Mothers' Union: a letter "To a priest on the death of an infant daughter", by Reginald Somerset Ward in *Death and Those We Love,* by Alix and George Reindorp.

A. R. Mowbray & Co. Ltd: *Widowhood,* by Joan Evelyn; *Spiritual Letters of Father Congreve, S.S.J.E.,* edited by W. H. Longridge.

The New American Library, Inc.: Plutarch's *Selected Essays on Love, the Family and the Good Life,* translated by Moses Hadas.

New Society (9 April 1964): "Grief as an Illness", by C. M. Parkes.

Peter Owen Ltd: *A Death in the Family,* by James Agee.

Oxford University Press: *Some Lambeth Letters,* edited by F. S. Temple.

Pastoral Psychology and the Reverend William F. Rogers, ph.d.: "Needs of the Bereaved", by William F. Rogers, in *Bereavement —Death—The Funeral,* edited by Simon Doniger.

The Reader's Digest (January 1964): "Help in Time of Sorrow".

Routledge & Kegan Paul Ltd: *Human Relations and Hospital Care,* by A. Cartwright; *The Child's Discovery of Death,* by S. Anthony; *Widows and their Families,* by P. Marris.

Sheed & Ward Ltd: *The Spiritual Letters of Dom John Chapman,* o.s.b., edited by Dom Roger Hudleston, o.s.b.

Tavistock Publications for permission to quote from *The Child, the Family and the Outside World,* by D. Winnicott (abridged edition), Penguin Books.

Tavistock Publications, London, and Grune & Stratton, New York: *An Approach to Community Mental Health,* by Gerald Caplan.

Preface

This present volume has been written to serve as a companion to *The Pastoral Care of the Dying*, for priests and ministers of all denominations have before them unique opportunities of ministering to both the dying and the bereaved. Even if they are not called as frequently as they would wish to the former, it will always fall to their lot to uplift and succour the latter when officiating at the Burial Office.

In this ministry something far more is needed than a brief call on the bereaved family either before or after the funeral. In order to exercise effective pastoral care the priest should be familiar with some of the dynamic forces underlying bereavement and grief. In other words, not only must he be sensitive to the needs of those who mourn but also able to understand and evaluate these needs. This is of particular importance in an age in which uncertainty and bewilderment abound. The results of a survey undertaken by Mass-Observation in 1947 revealed that two of every five persons who said they believed in God were by no means sure there was any life after death, half of them being fairly convinced that there was not. A more recent Report (1965) entitled *The Television Audience and Religion*, carried out by Social Surveys (Gallup Poll) Limited, stated that 15 per cent of all churchgoers do not believe in life after death. Again, Gorer in his social survey *Death, Grief, and Mourning in Contemporary Britain* (Cresset Press 1965) reports that "a quarter of the population states firmly that they do not believe in a future life, and the same number is uncertain; of the remainder some 15 per cent say that they believe in a future life but have little idea what it will be

like; and the rest voice a series of unorthodox beliefs, with
no overt religious content" (p. 33). Little wonder that "for
the great majority of the respondents, the clergyman who
conducted the funeral was a technician hired to do his job
in much the same fashion as the undertakers or monumental
masons" (p. 40)!

As in the previous volume chapter 1 comprises an his-
torical survey dealing with the "art of consolation" literature from the Classics and the early Fathers of the Church.
In chapter 2 where the varied problems of the widow and
bereaved children are discussed, the writer was much
assisted both by conversation and correspondence with Mrs
Margaret Torrie, Founder of "Cruse Clubs". Mrs Torrie
most generously shared much of her experience in working
with widows and their families.

Dr C. Murray Parkes, M.D., D.P.M., of The Tavistock Institute of Human Relations, who himself has undertaken
much research into the problems of bereavement, read
through chapters 3, 4, and 5 in their original drafts, and gave
much help and guidance in their arrangement and composition. Miss Margaret Atkin, Senior Medical Social Worker at
The Hospital for Sick Children, Great Ormond Street, was
also kind enough to read chapter 4. To all these friends who
helped in the compilation of this work I express my gratitude, at the same time insisting that I am alone responsible
for the views expressed and whatever shortcomings are
evident.

The information contained in PART TWO: "The Funeral
Director" is taken from *The Manual of Funeral Directing*,
and I wish to thank the National Association of Funeral
Directors for permission to quote the relevant sections. In
particular I owe a debt of gratitude to Mr Stanley E. Gill-
man, a former President of the Association, who was most
interested in the work undertaken and spared time to discuss together further co-operation between priest and
funeral director.

PART THREE forms a collection of "Spiritual Letters of

Consolation" drawn from the spiritual writers of the past and present.

My father, the Reverend A. J. Autton, and Miss Allan, Church House, Westminster, assisted in the task of type-writing the manuscript, and I much appreciate their readiness to undertake so laborious a task. I am most grateful to my publishers, S.P.C.K. for their co-operation and encouragement, and for their permission to quote from an earlier publication on the same theme—*Death and Bereavement*, S.P.C.K. Christian Knowledge Booklet (1965). Miss Allan also kindly corrected proofs, and my son, Michael, and my daughter, Mary, helped to compile the Index.

The writer is only too aware that it is those who have suffered the pangs of bereavement themselves who are the true comforters. After all, it is only they who can say in all honesty, "I know exactly how it feels. I have been through it all myself!" Some words of Austin Farrer come to mind. "It seems no consolation", he writes, "to say that good will one day come. You must be able to say that divine hope can temper human grief. Any Christian can say the first, only a sufferer can venture the second" (*Love Almighty and Ills Unlimited*, Collins 1962).

St George's Hospital, London, S.W.1.   NORMAN AUTTON
Feast of St Michael and All Angels,
29 September 1965

PART ONE

The Care of the Bereaved

They that love beyond the world cannot be separated by it. Death cannot kill what never dies. Nor can spirits ever be divided that love and live in the same divine principle; the root and record of their friendship.

Death is but crossing the world as friends do the seas; they live in one another still. For they must needs be present that love and live in that which is omnipresent. In this divine glass they see face to face; and their converse is free as well as pure. This is the comfort of friends, that though they may be said to die, yet their friendship and society are, in the best sense, ever present, because immortal.   WILLIAM PENN

At times when you are sad and upset, do not abandon the good works of prayer and penance which you have been in the habit of doing. The devil will try to unsettle you and persuade you to abandon them, but rather than this you should do more of them than usual and you will see how quickly the Lord comes to your aid.

ST TERESA OF AVILA

Then I saw a new heaven and a new earth, for the first heaven and the first earth had vanished, and there was no longer any sea. I saw the holy city, new Jerusalem, coming down out of heaven, made ready like a bride adorned for her husband. I heard a loud voice proclaiming from the throne: "Now at last God has his dwelling among men! He will dwell among them and they shall be his people, and God himself will be with them. He will wipe every tear from their eyes; there shall be an end to death, and to mourning and crying and pain; for the old order has passed away!"

Then he who sat on the throne said, "Behold! I am making all things new!"

Revelation of St John the Divine (N.E.B.)

Bring us, O Lord God, at our last awakening into the house and gate of heaven to enter into that gate and dwell in that house, where there shall be no darkness nor dazzling, but one equal light; no noise nor silence, but one equal music; no fears nor hopes, but one equal possession; no ends nor beginnings, but one equal eternity; in the habitations of Thy glory and dominion, world without end. Amen.   JOHN DONNE

1

The Art of Consolation

O Divine Master, grant that I may not so much seek to be
consoled as to console.... *A Prayer of St Francis*

How blest are the sorrowful; they shall find consolation.
Matt. 5.4 (N.E.B.)

Praise be to the God and Father of our Lord Jesus Christ,
the all-merciful Father, the God whose consolation never
fails us! He comforts us in all our troubles, so that we in
turn may be able to comfort others in any trouble of theirs
and to share with them the consolation we ourselves receive
from God. *2 Cor. 1.3,4 (N.E.B.)*

As the art of dying inspired a literature all of its own, so,
too, a literary genre came into being as a result of the
ancient consolatory letters and essays written to comfort
those in sorrow. Most common were the poetic *consolationes*
—for example, Ovid's "Ad Liviam" and Juvenal's Satire
XIII, but we shall confine our survey to extracts from Latin
and Greek prose.

The earliest examples can be associated with the ancient
schools of philosophy, but the first to give this type of literature definite form was the Academic philosopher, Crantor
(d. 268 B.C.), a native of Soli in Cilicia and a pupil of
Xenocrates. In his περὶ πένθους (*de consolatione*), written
to comfort a father on the deaths of his children, Crantor
strongly opposed the Stoic ideal of the rejection of the
emotions— ἀναλησία —stating categorically, "I do not in
the least agree with those who are so loud in their praise of
that sort of insensibility which neither can nor ought to

exist. Let me escape illness: should I be ill, let me have the capacity for feeling I previously possessed, whether it be knife or forceps that are to be applied to my body. For this state of apathy is not attained except at the cost of brutishness in the soul and callousness in the body."[1] Moderation in grief was the lesson taught by Crantor, for men should neither be insensible (ἀπαθεῖς) nor should they be oversensible (δυσπαθεῖς).

Cicero was much influenced by this early work of Crantor's, and in his *Academica* (ii.135) relates that "we have all read the Old Academician Crantor's *On Grief*, for it is not a large but a golden little volume and one to be thoroughly studied word by word". The earliest Latin examples of the consolatory literature are the Letters of Cicero. The two most important of these are Letter XVI, written to Titius probably from Rome *c.* 46 B.C., and Letter V written by Servius Sulpicius Rufus to Cicero from Athens, March, 45 B.C.

In the first Cicero writes about one form of consolation

extremely common-place, I grant you, which we ought always to have on our lips and in our hearts—to remember that we are human beings, born under a law which renders our life a target for all the slings and arrows of fortune, and that it is not for us to refuse to live under the conditions of our birth, nor to resent so impatiently the misfortunes we can by no process of forethought avoid, but, by recalling to mind what has befallen others, to induce the reflection that what has happened to ourselves is nothing new.... if you can rid yourself of this one idea that any evil, as you suppose, can have befallen those you loved, it means a very material abatement of your grief.

Rufus writes in no uncertain terms to console Cicero in his sorrow over the loss of his daughter, Tullia.

Tell me [he states] can it be for her that you are grieving? How many times must you yourself have reflected—and the thought has often occurred to me—that in these times theirs is not the most cruel fate who have been permitted painlessly to make the change from life to death? ... Never forget that you are Cicero, one who has ever been wont to instruct and advise others; and do not imitate bad physicians who, in treating the diseases of others, profess to have mastered the whole art of healing, but themselves they cannot cure; nay, rather apply to yourself and set before your own mind the precepts you so often seek to impress upon others.... We have observed on several occasions that you bear good fortune with admirable self-control and thereby gain much credit; make a point of convincing us at last that you can bear misfortune equally well, and that you do not think your burden heavier than you ought to think it, and so remove the impression that of all the virtues, this is one you lack.[2]

Cicero himself wrote a *Consolatio* to relieve his own grief over the loss of Tullia who had died at the early age of thirty-two. This work has now been lost, but we have extracts still remaining from quotations in his *Tusculan Disputations* (I.xxvii; I.xxxi; IV.xxix). He describes the work as one which "I composed (for I was no 'wise man') in the midst of mourning and grief, and I employed the remedy of which Chrysippus forbids the application to fresh ferments as it were of the soul, and did violence to nature in order that the strength of my grief might yield to the strength of the medicine". In his *Disputations* (III.xxxi) he outlines the duties of comforters, which are

to do away with distress root and branch, or allay it, or diminish it as far as possible, or stop its progress and not allow it to extend further, or to divert it elsewhere. There are some who think it the sole duty of a comforter to insist that the evil has no existence at all, as is the view of Cleanthes; some, like the Peripatetics, favour the lesson that the evil is not serious. Some again favour the withdrawal of attention from evil to good, as Epicurus does; some, like the Cyrenaics, think it enough to show that nothing unexpected has taken place. Chrysippus on the other hand considers that the main thing in giving comfort is to remove from the mind of the mourner the belief already described, in case he should think he is discharging a regular duty which is obligatory. There

are some too in favour of concentrating all these ways of ad-
ministering comfort ... pretty nearly as in my "Consolation"
I threw them all into one attempt at consolation; for my soul
was in a feverish state and I attempted every means of curing
its condition.[3]

Cicero goes on to remind us that the time factor is so important, for what Aeschylus describes as ἰατροὶ λόγοι
(healing words) should be spoken at the appropriate season.
Finding the only source of comfort in philosophy, Cicero
lists the remedial steps for the giving of comfort: (a) to show
that either there is no evil or very little; (b) to discuss the
common lot of life and any special feature that needs discussion in the lot of the individual mourner; (c) to show
that it is utter folly to be uselessly overcome by sorrow when
one realizes that there is no possible advantage. He can
place no reliability for comfort in the frequently repeated
phrase "You are not the only one"; it can be beneficial, "but
not always and not in all cases. For there are some who
scorn it, but it does make a difference how the remedy is
applied. For we have to point out how each of those who
bore his sufferings wisely, managed to bear them, and not
point out the inconvenience under which he laboured." As
the lawyers in court deal with individual cases, so we must
act "similarly in the alleviation of distress, for we have to
consider what method of treatment is admissable in each
particular case".

From the school of the Stoics we have Plutarch's (A.D. 46–
120) "Consolation to his Wife" and probably "Consolation
to Apollonius", although there is some doubt over its actual
authorship. The former was written on the death of his
little daughter, Timoxena, and is most moving and attrac-
tive, although lacking the Christian ethic. He sends the
letter to his wife whilst he himself is away from home, and
after the child's funeral. He knows he can be assured that
his wife has not indulged in any excesses and superstitions.

I was told [he writes] by those who were present and found
your conduct remarkable that you did not put on mourning

nor induce any uncomeliness or unseemliness in yourself or in your servants, that there was no preparation for extravagant solemnities at the grave, but that everything was done decently and quietly with only the family in attendance. . . . It is not only in bacchic celebrations that a virtuous woman must remain uncorrupted, but in sorrow too she must remember that excess is to be avoided and that transports of emotion require to be controlled; it is not her love, as the many think, that she must fight against, but the incontinence of her soul. Upon love we bestow sorrow and respect and an abiding memory of the departed; but the insatiable yearning for lamentation which leads to wailing and beating of the breast is no less shameful than unbridled voluptuousness—though men find it venial, for it is a bitter smart rather than an agreeable sensation which is associated with the impropriety.

Plutarch assures himself that his wife has kept clear of "the dreadful thing which does so much mischief in these cases—the visits of silly women and their cries and the continuing lamentations by which they fan and whet grief and prevent it from abating either through other causes or of itself . . . a man sunk in grief suffers every chance comer to stir and augment his affliction, like a running sore; and by reason of the fingering and consequent irritation it hardens into a serious and intractable evil. Against such a contingency I know that you will be on your guard."[4]

Lacking the literary standard of his "Consolation to his Wife", the letter, "Consolation to Apollonius", abounds in references and quotations from earlier works, and a number of similarities are apparent between this letter and Cicero's *Disputations*, which prompts one to believe that Plutarch shared Cicero's original source, namely Crantor's *de consolatione* (quoted in sections 3, 6, and 25). In expressing his sorrow over the death of Apollonius' son, he deems it unhelpful to urge premature composure "close upon the time of his death", for "even the best of physicians do not at once apply the remedy of medicines against acute attacks of suppurating humours, but allow the painfulness of the inflammation, without the application of external medicaments, to attain some assuagement of itself". It is good that grief should find some expression, "for I, for my part, cannot concur with those who extol that harsh and callous indifference, which is both impossible and unprofitable. For this will rob us of the kindly feeling which comes from mutual affection and which above all else we must conserve." Moderate indulgence seems to be the proper attitude to adopt. Plutarch sees that "reason is the best remedy for the cure of grief", for "one ought to realize, not merely that he himself is mortal by nature, but also that he is allotted to a life that is mortal and to conditions which readily reverse themselves. For men's bodies are indeed mortal, lasting but a day, and mortal is all that they experience and suffer, and, in a word, everything in life. . . ."

Another help suggested by Plutarch for those in bereavement is to realize that they are not alone in their sorrow. He refers his readers to one of the sayings of Socrates "which suggests that if we were all to bring misfortunes into a common store, so that each person should receive an equal share in the distribution, the majority would be glad to take up their own and depart". Antimachus after the death of his wife, Lyde, apparently composed an elegy "in which he enumerated the misfortunes of the heroes, and thus made his own grief less by means of others' ills. "So", suggests Plutarch, "it is clear that he who tries to console a person in grief, and demonstrates that the calamity is one which is common to many, and less than the calamities which have befallen others, changes the opinion of the one in grief and gives him a similar conviction—that his calamity is really less than he supposed it to be."

Far more important than the length of life is the quality of life, and "everyone ought to hold the conviction, if he seriously reviews the facts both by himself and in the company of another, that not the longest life is the best, but the most efficient. For it is not the man who has played the lyre the most, or made the most speeches, or piloted the most ships, who is commended, but he who has done these things excellently. Excellence is not to be ascribed to length of time, but to worth and timely fitness . . . we everywhere observe that it is a happy use of opportunity, rather than a happy old age, that wins the highest place . . . the measure of life is its excellence, not its length in years."

The remedy that seems to surpass all others for the alleviation of sorrow is that we are not to blame for our unhappy state. "It is a good thing, too", suggests Plutarch, "to call to mind the argument which most likely we have sometimes employed with relatives and friends who found themselves in similar calamities, when we tried to comfort them and to persuade them to bear the usual happenings of life in the usual way and a man's lot like a man . . . it is a good thing, too, to contemplate those men who nobly and highmindedly and calmly have been resigned to the deaths which have befallen their sons". . .[5]

The most famous of all the Stoics was Seneca (d. A.D. 65), and from his pen we have three *consolationes*—"Ad Marciam", "Ad Polybium", and "Ad Helviam", as well as some consolatory letters. His consolation to Marcia was written *c.* A.D. 37–41, and the other two dialogues were composed during Seneca's exile. The "Ad Helviam" takes the rather unique form for this literary genre in so far that Seneca, the mourned in exile, seeks to comfort his mother, Helvia, the mourner!

Marcia had lost both her father (Aulus Crematius Cordus, who committed suicide after being accused of treason under the Emperor Tiberius in A.D. 25) and two sons. Seneca writes to console her over the death of the one son, Metilius. In true Stoic style, Seneca tells Marcia in no uncertain terms that while "others deal with you gently and ply soft words . . . I myself have determined to battle with your grief, and your eyes that are wearied and worn— weeping now, if I may speak the truth, more from habit than from sorrow—shall be checked by measures that, if so it may be, you welcome, if not, even against your will, even though you hug and embrace the sorrow that you have kept alive in place of your son. . . ." Marcia is encouraged to "submit to conversation about your son . . . and let your ears be open to his name and memory; and do not consider this burdensome, after the fashion of some others, who in a calamity of this sort count it an added misfortune to have to listen to words of comfort." What can our grief do to help, argues Seneca. "If tears can vanquish fate, let us marshal tears; let every day be passed in grief, let every night be sleepless and consumed with sorrow; let hands rain blows on a bleeding breast, nor spare even the face from their assault; if sorrow will help, let us vent it in every kind of cruelty. But if no wailing can recall the dead, if no distress can alter a destiny that is immutable and fixed for all eternity, and if death holds fast whatever it has once carried off, then let grief, which is futile, cease." Anticipating Marcia's reactions to such sentiments, Seneca continues, "But, you say, Nature bids us grieve our dear ones. Who denies it, so long as grief is tempered?" responds the writer. "For not only the loss of those who are dearest to us, but a mere parting, brings an inevitable pang and wrings even the stoutest heart. But false opinion has added something more to our grief than Nature has prescribed. Observe how passionate and yet how brief is the sorrow of dumb animals . . . nor does any creature sorrow long for its offspring except man—he nurses his grief, and the measure of his affliction is not what he feels, but what he wills to feel."

In the dialogue to Polybius the same Stoic fortitude is impressed upon the mourner, although Seneca is not so strict as the earlier Stoics were—"I know well that some men are to be found whose wisdom is harsh rather than brave, who deny that the wise man will ever grieve . . . never will I demand of you that you should not grieve at all". Grief is all right for a limited time. "Let your tears flow, but let them also cease, let deepest sighs be drawn from your breast, but let them also find an end". Polybius is encouraged to think of all the good qualities of his departed brother—"Think of his modesty, think of his alertness in the activities of life, of his diligence in performing them, of his steadfastness to promises. Set forth all his words and deeds to others, and do you yourself recall them to mind."

dying of tears

Seneca's "Consolation to Helvia his Mother" seems to smack "of the cleverness of Stoic paradox and is, on the whole, more ingenious than convincing" as it develops the theme that neither Seneca nor Helvia are to be considered really unfortunate.[6] He reminds his mother that "our ancestors, seeking to compromise with the stubbornness of a woman's grief by a public ordinance, granted the space of ten months as the limit of mourning for a husband. They did not forbid their mourning, but limited it ... the best course is the mean between affection and reason—both to have a sense of loss and to crush it." He commends to his mother as a sure relief from her sorrow "philosophic studies", for "they will heal your wound, they will uproot all your sadness ... they will render you safe. They will comfort you, they will cheer you; if in earnest they gain entrance to your mind, never more will sorrow enter there, never more anxiety, never more the useless distress of futile suffering ... Philosophy is your most unfailing safeguard, and she alone can rescue you from the power of Fortune."[7]

In Seneca's *Ad Lucilium Epistulae Morales* we have two letters on grief and bereavement which are worth quoting. Letter LXIII is on "Grief for Lost Friends", and the writer confesses that it is often beyond one's power to desist altogether from weeping, "unless he has already risen far above the reach of Fortune", but we must see that "our tears have not flowed to excess". "Let not the eyes be dry when we have lost a friend, nor let them overflow. We may weep, but we must not wail". His other Letter XCIX, "On Consolation to the Bereaved", again stresses the futility of grief and puts forward three arguments. "In the first place it is idle to grieve if you get no help from grief. In the second place, it is unfair to complain about what has happened to one man but is in store for all. Again, it is foolish to lament one's loss when there is such a slight interval between the lost and the loser. . . ."[8]

One of the early Christian examples of the consolatory literature is found in St Basil (d. A.D. 379) and there are some four letters of his which deserve attention. The first is "To Nectarius in Consolation" in which he reminds the reader of the utterance of Job in the midst of his extreme sorrow—"The Lord gave and the Lord hath taken away; as it hath pleased the Lord, so is it done." Then Basil brings solace in the following words: "Let us make these marvellous words our own; equal is the reward at the hands of the righteous Judge for those who exhibit equally noble deeds. We have not been bereft of the boy, but we have given him back to the lender; nor has his life been destroyed, but merely transformed for the better; earth has not covered our beloved one, but heaven has received him. Let us abide a brief space, and we shall be with him whose loss we mourn."

Letter VI is addressed "To the Wife of Nectarius in Consolation". Basil stresses that she spare her partner in life— "Be a consolation one to the other; do not make the misfortune harder for him to bear by spending yourself upon your grief", and leads Nectarius' wife to prayer. "I believe", he writes, "that there is need of prayer also to meet this affliction. Therefore I do pray the Lord himself so to touch your heart with his ineffable power as to enkindle light in your soul by the exercise of good counsels, that you may have within yourself the sources of your consolation."

St Basil writes in A.D. 377–8 "To the Wife of Arinthaeus, the General, in Consolation" (Letter CCLXIX). Arinthaeus had been killed in Constantius' battle waged against the invading Goths in North Italy. Without waiting for the Emperor's orders, he, along with two other officers, made an attack which helped to turn seeming defeat into victory. Here the widow is shown the help of the Scriptures for those in sorrow. For "on all occasions the teaching of the Scriptures is helpful, but especially on such as these. Remember therefore the declaration of him who created us, according to which all of us who are of the dust shall return again to the dust; and no one is so great as to show himself superior to the dissolution."

Letter CCI is addressed "To Maximus", and contains reference to the Resurrection: "Above all, let the doctrine of the resurrection cheer your soul, since you are a Christian and pass your life in hope of the blessings to come. . . . Thus, therefore, you should think of her—as having gone her way by a certain road which we too shall have to travel; and if as having gone before us, this is not a matter worthy of tears."[9]

The funeral orations of St Gregory Nazianzen (d. A.D. 390) as well as those of St Ambrose are wonderful examples of Christian faith and Ciceronian rhetoric, and Gregory's panegyrics on his brother Caesarius (A.D. 369), on his sister Gorgonia, on his father and St Basil (A.D. 379), and Ambrose's orations on the Emperors Valentinian II and Theodosius, all indicate that the restraint of grief was not a universally accepted teaching among early Christians. In one of his letters (XXXIX) St Ambrose seeks to rouse Faustinus from excessive grief for his sister's death, and warns him not to "make her sorrowful by our tears", but "rather commend her soul to God by oblations".[10]

Perhaps one of the finest of the ancient letters of consolation comes from the pen of St Jerome (c. A.D. 345), written to Heliodorus, Bishop of Altinum, to console him on Nepotian's death, A.D. 396. The writer himself is quite overcome with grief, which he is not ashamed to reveal. "My heart is numbed, my hand trembles, my eyes are misty, my tongue stammers. All that I say seems voiceless, for he no longer hears. My very pen is rusty as though it felt his loss, my wax tablet looks dull and is covered over with mould . . . my eyes fill with tears, my pain begins again to rankle, and I can think of nothing but his death . . . though I struggle and try and fight against them, the tears still run down my cheeks; in spite of virtue's teaching and our hope of the

resurrection a passion of regret is breaking my fond heart.
O death that partest brothers and dost unknit the closest
bonds of love, how cruel art thou and how stern!" The two
aspects of sadness and joy are most wonderfully described
by St Jerome in the following terms which are worth
quoting at length.

We know, indeed, that our dear Nepotian is with Christ, and
that he has joined the choirs of the saints. We know that
what here with us on earth he groped after at a distance and
sought by guess-work, there he sees face to face and can say:
"As we have heard so we have seen in the city of the Lord of
hosts, in the city of our God" (Ps. 48.8). But we cannot bear
our regret at his absence, and we grieve not on his account but
for ourselves. The greater his happiness, the deeper our pain
in lacking the blessings that he enjoys. The sisters of Lazarus
wept for their brother, although they knew that he would
rise again, and the Saviour himself, to show that he possessed
true human feelings, mourned for the man he was going to
raise. . . . I beg you, however, to set a limit to your grief and to
remember the saying: "Nothing too much". Bind up your
wound for a little while, and listen to the praises of him in
whose virtue you always delighted. Do not grieve that you
have lost such a paragon, but rather rejoice that he once was
yours.[11]

The same notes of joy and sadness are apparent in the
early Burial Offices of the Church. Sorrow there will be, for
death means separation and loss, but joy there should be,
for "the Redemption demands that the Alleluia of triumph
shall be louder than the Amen of resignation". St Cyprian
reproved excessive mourning which was unchristian and
gave the heathen opportunity to pour scorn on belief in the
resurrection. "How often has it been revealed to us", he
writes in his *De Mortalitate* (c. xx), "that our brothers who
have been released from the world by the Divine summons
ought not to be mourned for, since we know that they are
not lost but gone before; while appearing to lose they have
really gained ground, as travellers and navigators are wont
to do." St Ambrose insists that "there ought to be some

difference between believers and unbelievers ... between
the servants of Christ and the worshippers of idols". Yet
death has its sorrowful aspects, for the Lord himself "wept
in that nature in which he was sad".[12] Christians were expected to wear white at funerals, and not the gloomy black
of the heathen.

Early Christian funerals were full of the symbolism of
victory. In the *Apostolic Constitutions*, a fourth-century
manual of Church Order, we have what is probably the
earliest account of a Christian funeral.

> Do not seek after Jewish separations [a reference to the defile-
> ment caused by contact with the dead], or perpetual washings,
> or purifications upon the touch of a dead body. But without
> such observances assemble in the cemeteries, reading the holy
> books, and singing psalms for the martyrs which are fallen
> asleep, and for all the saints from the beginning of the world,
> and for your brethren that are asleep in the Lord. Offer the
> acceptable Eucharist, the antitype of the royal body of Christ,
> in your churches, and in the cemeteries; and in the funerals of
> your dead lead them forth with psalms, if they were faithful
> in the Lord. For "Precious in the sight of the Lord is the
> death of his saints", and again, "Turn, my soul, unto thy rest;
> because the Lord hath done me good." And in another place,
> "The memory of the just is with praises, and the souls of the
> just are in the hand of God" (6.30).

Writing on the burial rites of the early Church, Plumptre[13]
describes how

> the Christian Church gave to the funeral procession somewhat
> of the character of a triumph. Those who took part in it
> carried in their hands branches of palm and olive, as those
> who celebrated victory. They strawed over the body leaves of
> laurel and ivy, the emblems of immortality; they carried
> lighted lamps or torches in like token of Christian joy; frag-
> rant clouds of incense rose, as in a Roman triumph. They did
> not march in sad silence to the grave ... but they chanted as
> they went hymns of hope and joy. The "hearty thanks" which
> we give to God at the grave for the deliverance of our

departed friends out of the miseries of this sinful world are, as it were, a faint echo of those old funeral anthems and psalms of the early Church.

The early Christian funeral was linked to a celebration of the Eucharist, uniting the Church Militant with the Church Triumphant. Eusebius in his *Vita Constantini* (iv. 71), describes the burial rites performed over Constantine in the church of the Apostles at Constantinople and relates how "he was honoured by the performance of the sacred ordinances and mystic liturgy..." At the burial of St Augustine's mother, Monica, in A.D. 387, "the Sacrament of our ransom was offered for her, as the manner is, while the corpse was by the side of the grave, previous to being laid therein".[14]

The Roman Sacramentaries offered a series of Masses for the departed not only on the actual day of burial but also for anniversaries, and Requiem Mass (*requiem aeternam dona eis, Domine*) held a regular place in the burial rites. As the years passed, "more and more the avenging judgement dominates the thought of death ... friends still carried torches of candles; incense was still swung in front of the body. But it was no longer a triumphant procession; it was a doleful cortège. The mourners were not dressed in white, but in black, as was the coffin. The psalms sung were penitential, the 'Miserere' being conspicuous among them."[15]

At the compilation of the First Prayer Book of Edward VI, drawn very largely from the services for the "Commendation of the Soul" and the "Burial of the Dead" in the Sarum Manual, drastic revisions in the ancient burial offices were made, but the Eucharist was maintained. The 1549 "Ordre for the Buriall of the Dead" consisted of the Procession, the Burial, an office of the Dead, and "The Celebracion of the holy communion when there is a burial of the dead". The Introit is Psalm 42; the Collect is "O merciful god the father of oure lorde Jesu Christ, who is the resurrection and the life; In whom whosoeuer beleueth shall liue thoughe he dye . . ."; the Epistle is from 1 Thess. 4; and the Gospel, John 6.

In the revision of 1552, all the prayers of the dead were omitted, and also the Holy Communion (apart from the Collect). There was even no provision made for any service in church at all. Attempts were made to remedy the omission of the Eucharist, and in 1560 Queen Elizabeth issued a Latin Prayer Book for use in the Universities and at Winchester and Eton, in which was appended a "Celebration of the Lord's Supper at funerals, if the friends and neighbours of the persons wish to communicate". The Collect, Epistle, and Gospel of the 1549 Book were brought back into use.

In the 1662 Prayer Book much was also restored of the original form, but still the Eucharist was omitted, and here again attempts were made in the later 1928 revision to bring back the Celebration,[16] as well as providing three new prayers for the departed and those who mourn, etc.

The revised Order for the Burial of the Dead as proposed in the Report of the Church of England Liturgical Commission to the Archbishops of Canterbury and York, October, 1964, makes provision for Communion to be celebrated. The Commission states "that such a remembrance seems to be particularly fitting on an occasion when there is need for mourning to be tempered with joy in what Christ has done for us and wills to accomplish in us".

As the Christian funeral should be dominated by the themes of joy and sadness,[17] so, too, must our consolation include the themes of sorrow and assurance. There can be no hard and fast rules for the art of consolation, for it can only be practised aright by those who are most sensitive to the needs of others, and very few would deny its extreme difficulties. As someone has so aptly put it, *ex cathedra* statements are poor substitutes for those which spring *ek kardias*.

There are, however, certain basic principles which can serve as helpful guides when we attempt to comfort and console those who are in bereavement:

3

1 All who mourn are best helped when they are led to face the reality of what has happened. *Sadness and sorrow* must be confronted before comfort will ensue. The words we utter or the letter of consolation we write should relate to the situation as it really is. The loss and separation must be looked at realistically. Death should be seen as "death" and shorn of euphemisms, thereby affording those who sorrow an opportunity to mourn.

2 They can be led to the resources which the Christian faith offers at a time when they are able to appreciate it and so be helped by it. The realization of the presence of God will remind them that they do not face their sorrow in their own strength, for "God himself shall be with them, and be their God". *Consolation and comfort* will be derived from the reading of the Scriptures, the assurance of the prayers of the faithful, the grace of the Sacraments, the certainty of the Resurrection, and the fellowship of the Communion of Saints.

These two guiding principles find wonderful illustration in one of the letters of consolation quoted on pp. 171f, where one priest who "during his lifetime ... gave himself wholly to the spiritual direction of souls, leading them on the way to God"[18] writes to comfort a fellow-priest and his wife on the death of their baby daughter. He begins: "It was with great sorrow that I heard to-day of the death of your child. The religion of Christ was always sincere and clear-sighted. He refused *to obscure the fact that tragedy was tragedy*; and wept at the grave of Lazarus ..." Here at the very commencement is the reader brought face to face with the fact of the "death of your child". No euphemisms are used; there are no attempts at explanation. "Torn hearts" are referred to at the loss of so young a child .The writer moves on to describe his own vision of what happens to the departed. ... "the companionship which was given you, you still have. The growth to which you look forward will still be yours to watch over and care for." Then comes assurance of the writer's prayers, believing as he does with firm conviction that "here in time and space, *grief and hope* can come to us side by side ..." (italics my own). Such a letter deserves careful study and meditation.[19]

In our hours of sadness and gloom we find true consolation in the fact that

> there will be sorrow in any Christian life—godly sorrow, not depression and despair and low spirits; but godly sorrow, the very sorrow of Jesus, who was sad in the presence of death and of the sufferings of mankind; godly sorrow, in which, as it were, we put our tiny drops of sorrow into that cup of sorrow which our Lord drained to the dregs. But there is joy—joy in the knowledge of redemption ... joy in the communion of saints, our brothers and sisters in Christ; the joy that comes from obedience.... There is, too, the joy of anticipation, the looking into heaven, hearing our Lord's invitation, "Come!" ... Our Lord said, "I go to prepare a place for you", "If it were not so, I would have told you", "that where I am ye may be also". This is the ultimate joy which eases the sorrows we must bear.[20]

2

The Fatherless and Widows

That it may please thee to defend and provide for the fatherless children, and widows, and all that are desolate and oppressed... *Litany, Book of Common Prayer*

Let not widows be neglected. Next to the Lord be yourself their guardian. *Ep. to Polycarp, IV.I*

The kind of religion which is without stain or fault... is this: to go to the help of orphans and widows in their distress. *James 1.27 (N.E.B.)*

THE FATHERLESS

In one of Katherine Mansfield's short stories, *At the Day*, Kezia and her grandmother are taking their siesta together, when the young child asks, "Why did Uncle William have to die? He wasn't old." Mrs Fairfield began counting the stitches in threes. "It just happened", she said in an absorbed voice. "Does everybody have to die?" asked Kezia. "Everybody." "Me?" Kezia sounded fearfully incredulous ... It is probably quite impossible for an adult really to imagine the intensity of feelings which a small child experiences when face to face with death. In the Victorian era death occurred frequently in the majority of homes, and children came face to face with the fact of death far more realistically than is the case to-day. The churchyard was in the heart of every village community and the funeral cortège was attended by much pomp and ceremony. Death was seen as something quite natural, and the young came to know it gradually as a normal function of life.

The common tendency at the present time is for parents to shield their children as much as possible from all contact with death or bereavement, for it is considered kinder that they be spared all the emotional upset and be shielded from the family grief. At the time of the funeral young children are usually sent off to friends and relations, who attempt to divert their attention from the sad event. On their return home very little is done to satisfy their curiosity. They are not encouraged to ask questions, and when they do they are fobbed off with trite remarks. Writing on "The British Way of Death" in the *Sunday Times Weekly Review* (15 November 1964), Geoffrey Gorer stated that many of the parents he interviewed "treated the subject as literally unmentionable". Such secrecy among children seems capable, he suggests, "of producing a number of very undesirable consequences, including the furtive excitement engendered by 'horror comics' and 'X' Films—the pornography of death". In an article on the "Maturation of Concepts of Death" (*British Journal of Medical Psychology* 39, 1966, p. 35), A. Maurer writes, "Holsters are strapped on toddlers before their second Christmas, yet when grandfather dies, hush, hush, hypocrisy requires that the child be told that grandfather just went to sleep."

Like adults, children who have lost someone whom they have held dear go through periods of mourning. Bowlby describes three phases of reaction to the loss of a loved one.[1] First there is PROTEST, for the child has been so used to mother responding to his cries, and now there is apt to be confusion and fright when his expectations are unfulfilled. Consequently he will often cry out loudly for help. A state of DESPAIR follows when an increasing sense of hopelessness overwhelms the child. He becomes withdrawn and apathetic, and seems to be in a state of deep mourning, weeping monotonously and intermittently. Finally there is DENIAL, as he begins to make the best of the situation by repressing his feeling for mother.

As soon as they sense that their parents fear death and

that the subject must never be discussed together in conversation, their own anxieties become intensified and they
have no one about them with whom they can talk about
things that disturb and puzzle them. If preparation and instruction form part of the normal upbringing of the child,
then he is a little more equipped when a death occurs within the family circle. Obviously there will still be grief when
loss is encountered, but at least there will be freer expression and the resolving of many emotional anxieties. When
one of the family pets dies—the dog or the cat, for example
—he can be led to see the naturalness of death.[2] Later he
will be able to share a little in the sorrow and sadness of the
family, and not feel excluded and shut off from something
which is dark and foreboding. When he is allowed to share
his parents' grief, he acquires a sense of fulfilment; a realization that there are things he can do to help. He senses he
now has a part to play, a right to belong, and he will often
emerge enriched and unharmed. Such a cathartic process
will be completely inhibited if the parents attempt just to
carry on as if nothing had happened and hope that the
child will probably forget.

If children are fed on half-truths much harm will ensue
in later life. They can stand "tragedy, sorrow, tears much
better than they can stand lies, deceit, evasions". They can
face "tears but not treachery, sorrow but not deceit".[3]

A most helpful study on "The Child's View of Death"
has been undertaken by Maria H. Nagy.[4] Data were com-
piled from 378 children living in Budapest and its environs.
The group was equally divided—51% boys, 49% girls, and
ages ranged from 3–10 years. They represented various re-
ligions, schools, and social background. The study was
carried out in the following manner: (a) children in the
7–10 age group were asked to write a composition in answer
to the statement, "Write down everything that comes to
your mind about death"; (b) the 6–10 age group were in-
vited to do drawings about death, and the older children
were then asked to write explanations of the drawings; (c)

discussions took place with all the children involved about the work they had done both in their drawings and essays.

As a result of these studies, Maria Nagy was able to categorize three major stages.

1 Children under five usually do not view death as an irreversible fact, for "in death he sees life". Death seems a sort of departure or sleep. Some of the compositions and discussions implied that if the dead do go away they are still alive wherever they might be. "A dead person is just as if he were asleep. Sleeps in the ground, too", was the remark of a child of four years and ten months. This conception of death as sleep is also borne out in the study made by Sylvia Anthony[5] in which she relates how a little girl of three "was alone with her mother at home, when the mother, as she was making a bed, suddenly fell upon the floor and apparently died instantly of heart failure. The father returned to find the mother dead, and the little girl asleep on the floor beside her. The little girl, four months later, relating the event to her teacher quite happily remarked, "Mother lay down on the floor and went to sleep, so I went to sleep too."

2 From the age of five to nine years children often personify death. An increased sense of the reality begins to make an appearance at this stage. Death exists "but it is remote from us. As it is remote our death is not inevitable. Only those die whom the death-man catches and carries off. Whoever can get away does not die." This idea of the "death-man" seems to be deeply imbedded in primitive tribal thinking.

3 It is only when they reach the age of nine years and onwards that children see death as an event which occurs in accordance with certain laws. Nagy emphasizes the difficulty of classification at this young age, for much overlapping can occur. However, the predominant features of the older group appear to be the inevitability and universality of death. One child of nine years and four months

expresses it this way: What is death? Well, I think it is part of a person's life. Like school. Life has many parts. Only one part of it is earthly. As in school, we go on to a different class. To die means to begin a new life. Everyone has to die once, but the soul lives on." (Out of the mouths of babes . . . !)

In the sharing of bereavement obvious discretion must be exercised by parents in circumstances which vary from family to family. If parents are suffering acute grief, very young children are better away from the environment, for such a traumatic experience may do them more harm than good. One of their greatest problems is "to feel that the adults like father and mother who seem so big and important and powerful in his eyes, can be powerless in the face of death, and this can give rise to many baffling and anxious thoughts".[6] Where normal reactions to grief are encountered, it is better for the child to take his place as a member of a sorrowing family during their period of mourning.

When opportunities occur to prepare a child for an expected death, it should be done with as much tact and discretion as possible. Pauline Best relates how this might be done in a most helpful article which provides valuable material for both priest and parent.[7] Billy, aged five years, had died during the night after a brief illness. The news came through only thirty minutes before class was about to assemble. As soon as Billy was missed by his class-mates, Miss Best, their teacher, quietly told them that "Billy won't be here to-day—I will tell you why after a while". The class are then asked if they know what will happen to them when they die. Some of their thoughts were couched in the following terms. "God takes dead people to live with him, but we don't know how." "We don't know, but God loves you whether you are dead or alive." It is at this stage that their teacher breaks the news of Billy's death to the class. After a short silence a third-grade child speaks up. "He was a nice little boy, wasn't he!", and a first-grade asks, "Did his mother cry?" After a further series of comments, Miss Best states that "perhaps there are other things you would like to say about Billy, and we could tell them to his mother, so she would know how we feel". After compiling a short list —for example, Billy always came on time, Billy liked to sing, etc.—they were asked, "Do you know where Billy is to-day or what he is doing?" After some thought and not a little perplexity, one of the children remarked, "We don't know, but we do know God is loving him." Miss Best summarizes the situation for them, emphasizing the fact that God loves Billy and is taking care of him, and this prompts one small child to respond, "We don't have to worry about him, do we?" To which their teacher replies, "No, we don't have to worry about him because God loves him. The things we remember about him are the part of Billy that is with God now. We miss Billy very much, but we can say prayers for him, and he can say prayers for us, just like we always do."

All that took place in the class that morning was described in a letter to Billy's parents. The day after the funeral his mother could state, "If children can see that so well, why do we adults make it so difficult for ourselves?" Some weeks later when the children were learning the doxology, they came to the words, "Ye heavenly host", and a six-year-old remarked rather wonderfully, "That means Billy, doesn't it?" All the other children agreed.

If death can be described in such terms as are understood by children, as in the class-room scene related above, much of the fear of dying is resolved. Helping them to recall the happy events in Billy's life was a major step in relieving much of their grief as well as that of Billy's mother. If the bereaved can be led to the happy positives of life together throughout their married life, both parents and children are helped. It is rather indicative of our present attitude to death that very few teachers would dare to talk to children in this way, yet how helpful such a discussion would be if developed not only in the classroom but also in the hospital ward or Church group. It is important that when death is explained to children it should be done in terms that are not only religiously valid, but also emotionally satisfying. It is not so much what is said but how it is said that is important, for words uttered at such a time live long in the child's memory, and they quickly sense the sincerity or otherwise of what is said during such highly emotional periods.

Unfortunately, some of the more common expressions used are not as helpful and satisfying as they might be. Indeed so many are positively harmful: "Jesus has taken him!" "God wanted her so he's taken her to Heaven." Gorer found that "people with no religious convictions of their own, who state explicitly that they do not believe in an after-life and never go to a place of worship, tell their children that the dead have "gone to heaven" or "gone to Jesus" and the like. "It is difficult", summarizes Gorer, "to avoid the conclusion that a sizeable minority of British parents are using God and Jesus in communication with their children in exactly the same way as they use Santa Claus." Indeed, one mother said that she "tried to make it as much like a fairy-story as possible".[8] One can well imagine the utter shock and bewilderment confronting the young child when his first disillusionment about Father Christmas occurs!

Even when the family has strong religious affiliations, the terms in which they can express death to their children become far too abstract, and represent to the child's mind a rather cruel, horrid sort of God who has taken his Mummy away. What a young child wants is not so much a mere theory or explanation of death, but far more important is a sense of reassurance and sustaining security. He can be told quite simply about the life to come where there will be no more pain or death, and where those who have died go on living in a different world and in a different form. Here is surely a time for the parents to get right away from the fairy-tale act and get right down to the depths of the Gospel, for the bereaved can then really enter into the very heart of Christ's compassion for suffering humanity, seen in his love for the fatherless and widows, for the sick in mind and body, and for those who are disturbed by "nightmares" like the man among the tombs.

It is not as helpful as it may sound to refer to "God's Will", for this may so easily arouse in the child's mind an anger against such a God and rebellion over such a cruel Will. He can also become terribly frightened, dreading that this same "Will" might be the cause of his own death. Such fears can lead to nightmares and aggressive and delinquent behaviour.

Parents help a child over bereavement most when they give him every available opportunity to express his feelings and fears. When this is done in a permissive atmosphere, he might easily recall an incident when in the midst of a temper tantrum he shouted, "I'd like to kill you", or "I wish you were dead!" Has his wish come true now, he wonders? Is he in any way responsible for the death that has occurred, he ponders? After all, he did say . . . he reflects. Although to an adult mind such fears are wholly unreasonable, he must remember that to the child they can be very real and terrifying, Adults are very guilty about their own aggressive feelings at such a time, and unless they understand this, they have very little resource to comfort the little child who feels that perhaps he has "killed" his parent. Much help and guidance is needed during these phases if both parent and child are going to find real comfort and consolation. The child must be allowed "to talk freely about things as he sees them, to ask questions and have them directly answered; then the sorrows he may still feel will tend to be perhaps of their kind no less deep, but devoid of that peculiar painfulness which attends remorse, and the morbidity that marks irrational remorse. He can be given the opportunity to talk about the person who has died, and should find that he may express hostility as well as love towards the dead."[9] He can be helped to understand that although there were times when he was naughty, Daddy perfectly understood, and that he loved him just as he was.

As well as blaming themselves, children can equally blame Mother for what has happened to Father, and might well feel that in some way she too has been responsible for what has happened. How a young child can be enabled to share in the family grief, and truth become an instrument of healing is related by Ilig and Ames,[10] in a letter written to the Gesell Institute. "My son died at five months of age, when my daughter was five years old. There are no other children. We found truth to be our most valuable asset. We allowed our little girl to participate in the truth with her eyes, ears, and body. The truth to her did not contain the elements of sorrow and grief that it did to us. She danced and sung and played her way through the tragic days of his death, service, and burial ... helping her to understand and accept the truth has had great benefit for me, her mother. Each time I had to search for simple language with which to explain to her. I found renewed strength in facing the Reality and Finality of what had happened ... with Truth as our guiding goal, we helped her and she helped me."

The timing element in the breaking of news about a death is of great importance. Uppermost in the child's mind will be anxiety, loneliness, and insecurity about the future, and "many of their indirect expressions will be asking for evidence that they will be taken care of. Their primary concern and insecurity may well come from not knowing or fearing what their father's death will do to them. This is the time when your children need you around them to re-assure them that their whole lives are not falling apart."[11] One of the most common anxieties of early childhood is the fear of separation. "Who will look after me now that Mummy has gone?" "Who will play with me now?" Who will reassure him when his mother's stability is beginning to rock and quaver? His prime need at this time will be to feel that there will be someone at hand to care for him and look after him, and here lies a challenge to the community, members of other families, the Church, Sunday school, and other organizations, to provide a motherly (or fatherly) person who will act as a parent substitute. It is important that such a person remain constant, for nothing can prove more bewildering and threatening to the child than a series of different people appearing in this rôle at various times. The companionship of other children either of his own age or older people will help him to gain a sense of support and security.

Methods of consolation will obviously vary according to age and temperament. The conception of death as a punishment for some wrong-doing in the past must be avoided at all costs, for it is essential that God be seen as a loving Father, as in the account of Billy at school, and the child's questions should be answered as honestly and frankly as possible. In postponing acceptance of death for their children many parents only succeed in postponing it for themselves. How well the parents work through their grief will have much to do with whether their children grow up with healthy or morbid ideas and thoughts of death. "Pretend" stories will always do a great deal of harm in the long run. A child is never indifferent and the wound goes very deep. As far as possible, let the parent discover what exactly is in the child's mind. Often a rather stunned reaction can be mistaken for sheer indifference. Again, he might have appeared to have forgotten all about mother or father, but to a watchful parent it is apparent that there are tensions and desires within.

No child should be coerced to react in a way preconceived by the parents. It is so very difficult for a youngster to "take in" the fact that "Daddy will never come back", for as we have already noted, he may realize the thought of deprivation, but irretrievable loss is quite beyond his grasp. After all, he is able to share but a small part of his parent's feelings, but what thoughts he has have to be valued and respected, as well as carefully handled by someone who is strong enough to uphold and support him.

An added threat to the child's security is the illness of the surviving parent. Sometimes the strain of bereavement can prove too hard a blow, and a mother is forced to take a rest. She might be admitted to hospital or to a nursing-home for medical or psychiatric care. Having already been deprived of his father, the child now begins to wonder whether Mother is going to leave him as well. His fears of insecurity will have to be watched, and friends and family will need the utmost understanding in handling what can be an extremely delicate situation. Mother's fears are in need of attention, too, of course.

Care must also be taken over the stress periods of the child's later life after bereavement has been experienced. These stages are felt more acutely when there is no father to approach for support and understanding. The emotional upheavals of adolescence, examinations, love affairs (where a jilting can revive a grief situation), are particularly sensitive areas which a wise parent might be able to anticipate and so help the child to face up to the difficulties involved.[12]

Finally, the problem of the suicide of the parent must be considered, more especially as rates of suicide now amount to approximately 5,000 a year. Here of course no natural death has occurred, and the realization that father took his own life must come as a most traumatic blow to the child. Father has gone off *of his own accord*! Why? The social stigma attached to the act prompts the family to withdraw with a strong sense of shame, and blame for the suicide might be levied from one to the other. Again, there are the jibes of school-mates to contend with, for these can do untold damage to a highly sensitive child. As he cannot blame God, he might think it was his mother's fault. Where mental illness has been the cause, the stability of the children will have to be watched and preventive care taken. Such a family needs all the care and support that a loving Church can offer it.[13]

THE WIDOWS

It has been estimated that in England and Wales alone there are some two and a half million widows, including half a million under the age of fifty-four. Of every five married women, one is a widow. To lose a husband is surely one of the most devastating blows that can befall one, especially when the widow is left with young children to bring up and support. Not only must she now adjust herself to the shock and strain of bereavement but also to a frightening sense of insecurity, for she has to fulfil a dual rôle in the family's life, becoming housekeeper, mother, and earner. Addressing the International Family Days Congress on "The Greatness of Widowhood", Pope Pius XII describes her situation in the following terms. "All of a sudden, the woman finds herself horribly alone, abandoned, bending under the burden of her sorrow and the responsibility she must face; how can she provide sustenance for herself and her children? How can she solve the cruel dilemma; how can she leave her dear ones or leave home to earn her daily bread? How can she preserve her rightful independence in spite of the necessary appeals for help to close relatives or even other families. It is enough to call to mind these questions to understand to what degree the widow feels dejected and sometimes rebels when faced with the immense bitterness which heaps itself upon her, and with the anguish which surrounds her like an unscalable wall."

The importance of a father's rôle within the family unit cannot be overemphasized. When a mother and a father share a happy and congenial relationship, the children feel safe and secure. Between two such parents young children are able to receive a balance of emotions and ideas and normally become contented and assured. Mother's love and care are essential and equally essential is father's moral support, "to be the backing for her authority, to be the human being who stands for the law and order which mother plants in the life of the child. He does not have to be there all the time to do this, but he has to turn up often enough for the child to feel that he is real and alive. Much of the arranging of a child's life must be done by mother ... but if she has to be the whole thing, and has to provide the whole of the strong or strict element in her children's lives as well as the love, she carries a big burden indeed ... every now and again the child is going to hate someone, and if father is not there to tell him where to get off, he will hate his mother, and this will make him confused, because it is his mother that he loves most fundamentally."[14] Bowlby in his *Child Care and the Growth of Love* shows what an important place a father has during the infant years of his children, for "not only do they provide for their wives to enable them to devote themselves unrestrictedly to the care of the infant and toddler, but, by providing love and companionship, they support the mother emotionally and help her maintain that harmonious contented mood in the atmosphere in which the infant thrives".[15]

Resulting from inner stress and emotional tension, there may follow periods of severe bitterness and a strong tendency to withdraw from the company of married couples. An acute sensitivity arising from reduced circumstances prompts the widow to give up former social contacts and shun public occasions. Consequently, unless help is forthcoming she can retreat into isolation and loneliness which brings further despair and gloom. This withdrawal might be seen as part of her mourning process, for in a society which places strong taboos on the expression of emotions there can be much misunderstanding and a complete lack of fellow-feeling. So often life can become a quandary, for if she "puts on" a brave face, the tendency of friends might be to interpret such reaction as signifying a lack of affection and love of the husband, while it can become so embarrassing and unseemly if she gives way to her feelings in public. The obvious solution to the difficulty of behaving in a natural way appears to be to retract from such threatening circumstances. She may be compelled to go out to work in order to sustain her family, and yet meet with criticism for neglecting and leaving her children. The community can sometimes be not only unhelpful but unkind.

One of the greatest difficulties confronting a widow with young children is the discipline of her offspring, especially when they are passing through the stage of adolescence. Felix Brown has shown how disturbances can arise after the loss of a parent during childhood,[16] after studying the cases of 216 unselected patients suffering from depressive illness attending Hampstead General Hospital Psychiatric Department. "If, as the statistics imply," writes Brown, "41 per cent of people suffering from depressive illness now lost a parent in the first fifteen years of their life, compared with 16 per cent in the general population, then it would seem that something should be done to prevent depressive illness by increased care of these orphans ... exactly how to prevent subsequent depressive illness in a bereaved child we do not know, but it seems reasonable to suppose that solicitude from surviving relatives, and an adequate parent substitute, provide the environment most conducive to recovery from childhood bereavement. The fact that the child at the time shows no obvious emotional disturbance is no evidence that he or she is not deeply affected, rather the reverse."[17]

If the mother is aware of some of the emotional readjustments which children have to make after the loss of a father, she will be better equipped to deal with some of the behaviour patterns which might arise later. The children might resent her when she has to fulfil her rôle as disciplinary agent. Things may become so strained and such periods so difficult that a mother may have an unconscious and forbidden wish that she would have been better off without the children. She might also well feel that she cannot find time to give them all the support and reassurance they need. Writing on "Widowhood", Joan Evelyn discloses some of the lessons she herself learnt from her bereavement, and confesses that "you face the fact that were it not for your children, you would be off exploring pastures new as a means of taking your mind off yourself and your unsatisfied sexual desires. Yes, children can be a great help, but they are not inevitably. Don't imagine you are the only woman who has ever felt like this; don't imagine you are 'wicked' because you do. Face the fact that you do feel this way and . . . as it hurts you, it will heal you."[18] A widow, in her attempt to seek comfort and consolation from her children, may become over-possessive and express excessive affection towards them. A son can become the object of the emotional satisfaction which the husband provided in the past, and such mother-fixation can lead on to frustration in the son's marriage or deprive him of any desire for marriage.

A son should have a father-substitute, for no matter how hard mother tries she can never become this, nor would it be right for her to try. He must be given full and free opportunity to mix with older boys and find for himself a father-figure in a teacher, club-leader, or scout-master, etc. Better still, if another family can take close interest in him so that he is given adequate support to venture forth into the world. Let him be encouraged to adopt a social and outgoing attitude toward life, without harbouring a keen sense of guilt for not being always at home.[19]

A daughter may find that the deprivation of a father makes it difficult for her to establish good relationships with men, and later there might arise the desire to marry a man much older than herself to compensate for the loss of a father's love and care. "Our job as mothers", writes Joan Evelyn, "is to help our children to want to grow up into the kind of people we wish them to be. So they must be given every opportunity of developing their own personalities without being attached to mother's apron strings. This, of course, is true in every family, but I believe it especially true when mother is single-handed. She is more likely to be wrongly possessive of her children when there is no one to give her a warning word."[20]

As well as social and emotional difficulties the widow can also encounter financial embarrassment, for pensions are still very small and inadequate, and the interaction of both financial and emotional problems needs a thorough understanding if help and compassion are to be forthcoming.[21]

The community care which the widow and the fatherless need offers a challenge to the Church of to-day. With its worshipping congregation, the "household of God" can play a vital therapeutic rôle, for those who mourn need empathetic care. Fortunate indeed are the widows who have the companionship and support of friends who understand and accept their moments of sadness and isolation.

One organization which is carrying out a pioneering counselling service for widows and their children is The Cruse Clubs. Founded by Mrs Margaret Torrie in 1958, it numbers among its aims and objects the following:

1. The relief of suffering and distress among widows and their children.

2. With a view to alleviating the isolation of widows and their sense of loneliness to assist the formation of Cruse Clubs and to organize visits between widows.

3. To collect and publish information about the Social Services, statutory or otherwise, and other matters which will be of benefit and assistance to widows.

4. To establish a panel of counsellors who will visit widows to advise and assist them.

5. To provide facilities for recreation and other leisure time occupation for widows in the interests of their social welfare as defined in the Recreational Charities Act, 1958 and as therein limited.

6. To undertake research into the special problems arising from widowhood and into the methods of alleviating suffering arising therefrom and to publish the results of such research.

7. To assist in providing holidays for widows who could not otherwise afford them.

8. To create and promote by publicity and education an informed and interested public opinion on the needs of widows, and also to publish a journal or other

means of disseminating information of assistance to widows in meeting their special needs.

Counselling is undertaken by trained caseworkers, and mixed group activities play an important part in the programme of the various Clubs throughout the country, as well as discussion groups and Parents Circles where the various problems of child management are worked through. That the need is great for both individual and group counselling is evidenced by extracts from widows' letters sent to the headquarters of the organization (Cruse Clubs, 6 Lion Gate Gardens, Richmond). "I have three daughters and although my free time is limited, the social ostracism is there all the time." "I lost my very dear partner last year and I feel as if only half of me is now left to carry on alone. The loneliness and emptiness of life has to be experienced to be believed. The future just seems void and blank to me at the moment." "I am a widow of a year with two little adopted girls of six and three years and have often felt in great need of help. So far I have been unable to find this, or any companionship, which is a great need, as the loneliness and problems of being left to bring children up, single-handed, are very great." "I now understand why friends, of whom I have always been very fond, stopped visiting me, and inviting me to their homes after I lost my husband. I must admit that I have felt very hurt about it."

Loneliness which a widow can feel when bereft not only of a husband but also of the companionship of friends, and in a non-caring community, is all too sadly shown in a suicide note left by an elderly widow[22]—"I find myself", she wrote, "in the unfortunate position of having to live entirely on my own. Until this happened, loneliness was just something I could not understand. Now I realize the full meaning of this terrible word, when I come back to the empty house, with no one to greet me, no one to talk to, no one with whom you can discuss the day's comings and goings." Let me implore friends of people who live alone not to forget them. Visit them, invite them to your homes. . . .[23]

Here lies a comparatively untouched sphere of pastoral care, where opportunities abound for further co-operation between priest, general practitioner, psychiatrist, social worker, and the welfare agencies, to relieve the loneliness and sufferings of the fatherless and widows. The loss of a husband can make one feel very much "out of it" when in the company of others, even when friends abound. It is not easy for the bereaved to face a situation which can often prove threatening and disturbing. Members of the congregation or of the various organizations within the Church can undertake to become a "caring" person, offering companionship, directing the conversation within the social group into channels which help and not hinder, and so facilitate mutual contacts. Group work among widows can be carried out within the various organizations, and an occasional sermon preached on death and the reactions of bereavement. Young Wives, Mothers' Unions, Men's Societies would do well to explore ways of making the lot of widows and orphans less forlorn and desolate.

What can be done on the parish level in a quiet and unassuming way is outlined by one clergyman thus:

> The bereaved person is usually surrounded by friends and cushioned by every comfort they can provide—*at first*. But what happens a few weeks later? The anaesthetic of his initial shock has worn off. The sad little tasks that kept him busy are all accomplished. The friends drift off to their own concerns. He is left alone too soon. Several years ago a widow in my congregation, with the help of three others, dedicated herself to getting people through what she called "the second phase of sorrow". It is the only secret society of which I am a member. What do we do? We invite the bereaved person to our homes on nights which would probably be heart-breaking—on anniversaries or birthdays and, of course, at Christmas. We try to provide and encourage hobbies. In one case we helped to arrange the adoption of a child for a woman who had lost her baby. None of these people suspects what we are doing. Later, when they are better adjusted, we invite them to become members. So far we have forty-six—a chain that is constantly growing, linked by a common need to comfort and be comforted.[24]

3

Normal and Abnormal Reactions to Grief

> Everyone can master a grief but he that has it.
> SHAKESPEARE: *Much Ado About Nothing*

> And the king was much moved, and went up
> to the chamber over the gate, and wept; and
> as he went thus he said, O my son Absalom, my
> son, my son Absalom! Would God that I had
> died for thee, O Absalom, my son, my son!
> *2 Sam. 18.33*

> We want you not to remain in ignorance,
> brothers, about those who sleep in death; you
> should not grieve like the rest of men, who have
> no hope. *1 Thess. 4.13 (N.E.B.)*

NORMAL REACTIONS

Grief is an emotion and a very painful one. As each individual is a rather unique personality, so each will differ in reactions to it. As Bowlby reminds us it

> is no respecter of persons. Whether the bereaved is young or
> old, rich or poor, to lose another with whom his feelings are
> closely linked is to suffer emotional disruption. Not only is the
> external pattern of his life abruptly changed, but he finds
> himself at the mercy of conflicting impulses of great intensity
> —to remember, to forget; to blame, to forgive; to seek com-
> panionship, to avoid company. No wonder this is an ex-
> perience which can endanger physical and mental health, both
> in the short-term and the long.... the problem is to under-
> stand the nature of the processes set in train by bereavement,
> and the conditions which assist these processes to reach a

healthy outcome or which hinder it; since without such understanding neither therapeutic nor preventive measures will be well-based.[1]

There are some persons who are strong-minded, and there are others who will be found to be abnormally sensitive, highly emotional, and over-dependent. Some will give vent to much sorrow, while others again will show little. Grief will often vary, too, according to circumstances. Normally the closer the relationship the more intense the grief. If the death of a loved one has been sudden, unexpected, or tragic, much emotional shock will follow, which seems to act as a temporary "anaesthetic". If the deceased had borne a long-continued illness with prolonged suffering, the process of bereavement might well have begun before the actual death has occurred. In this instance the period of acute grief might well be shorter and less intense. Indeed, there might be a sense of relief overshadowing the grief itself. Much will depend therefore upon particular circumstances of bereavement and upon each person's constitutional make-up.

Sigmund Freud in his study on "Mourning and Melancholia" noted that there was a marked similarity between mourners and melancholics. He discovered that both suffered from almost exactly the same symptoms—loss of interest, dejection, self-reproach, and self-punitive reactions. To Freud "mourning is regularly the reaction of the loss of a loved person", and he points out that "it never occurs to us to regard it as a morbid condition and hand the mourner over to medical treatment. We rest assured that after a lapse of time it will be overcome, and we look upon any interference with it as inadvisable or even harmful." If there is to be relief from grief "the work of mourning" has to be undergone. This is a painful task and is often resisted by the bereaved who cling to the illusion that the loved one still lives. "The struggle is so intense", Freud tells us, "that a turning away from reality ensues, the object being clung to through the medium of a hallucinatory wish-psychosis. The normal outcome is that deference for reality gains the day . . . the task is now carried through bit by bit, under great expense of time and cathartic energy, while all the time the existence of the lost object is continued in the mind."[2] Severing attachment to the "non-existent object" entails much intense struggle, and consequently very little energy is left for interest in the outer world. When the work of mourning has been completed, renewed freedom is found to carry on with one's normal life again.

Karl Abraham, in his study of depressed states, related the concept of the primal depression which occurred in infancy because of disappointment in obtaining the love of the mother to bereavement. Like Freud he saw a reactivation of this infantile depressive state in both normal and abnormal mourning.

Twenty years later Melanie Klein working on manic-depressive states also saw mourning as the working through of grief, and based her interpretations on the psychology of early childhood. Like Abraham and Freud, Klein suggests that the pathological bereaved person never seems to have outgrown the infantile depressive position. He never has been able to feel secure within, and when he is faced with bereavement or the loss of a love-object, all his insecurity and anxieties come to the surface. Memories of the loved one has to be revived several times before the mourner would be sufficiently free to relate normally to life again.

In Boston, Massachusetts, the great Coconut Grove Fire occurred in 1943. Many of the victims were admitted to Massachusetts General Hospital and treated by Dr Erich Lindemann, who was thus enabled to study at first hand the reactions of the survivors and families of the 101 victims who perished in the disaster. Many others were attended by him in the Grief Clinic he set up at that time. His "Symptomatology and Management of Acute Grief"[3] is among the most helpful of all studies on grief, and those who minister to the bereaved will find much here to help them.

The reactions of the acutely bereaved person are described by Lindemann in the following terms.

The activity throughout the day of the severely bereaved person shows remarkable changes. There is no retardation of action and speech; quite to the contrary there is a push of speech, especially when talking about the deceased. There is restlessness, inability to sit still, moving about in an aimless fashion, continually searching for something to do. There is, however, at the same time, a painful lack of capacity to initiate and maintain organized patterns of activity. What is done is done with lack of zest, as though one were going through the motions. The bereaved clings to the daily routine of prescribed activities; but these activities do not proceed in the automatic, self-sustaining fashion which characterizes normal work, but have to be carried on with effort, as though each fragment of the activity became a special task. The bereaved is surprised to find how large a part of his customary activity was done in some meaningful relationship to the deceased and has now lost its significance...

From these psychological studies we are now able to classify some of the reactions to grief which might be termed "normal" and "abnormal". Yet, any indiscriminate classification must be avoided at all costs, for so much is still complex. It must always be remembered that we are dealing with differing dispositions and temperaments. According to Lindemann "acute grief is a definite syndrone with psychological and somatic symptomatology", so we shall divide the reactions into physical and psychological.[4]

PHYSICAL

There may be uncontrollable crying and a shock-like state of confusion. A hollow feeling may occur in the stomach, difficulties in breathing and a loss of muscular power can follow. Arms and feet appear heavy and walking becomes irksome, although there may be the tendency to walk up and down in an aimless manner. A pounding and throbbing in the head and palpitation of the heart can be other symptoms, together with a need to sigh. A loss of appetite and sleep will be very marked. This is also borne out in Gorer's study *Death, Grief and Mourning in Contemporary Britain*, where he states that "two-thirds of the women mourners and two-fifths of the men stated that they slept less well after their bereavement than they did before; over half the bereaved population suffered from disturbed rest" (p. 53).

With some the urge to cry is suppressed, for it is still held to be humiliating and unmanly to express such emotions in public. Lindemann relates how "one of the big obstacles to this work seems to be the fact that many patients try to avoid the intense distress connected with the grief experience and the expression of emotion necessary for it. The men victims after the Coconut Grove Fire, for example, appeared in the early psychiatric interviews to be in a state of tension with tightened facial musculature, unable to relax for fear that they might 'break down'. It required considerable persuasion to yield to the grief process before they were willing to accept the discomfort of bereavement."

Another marked physical feature is lassitude of mind and body. The bereaved are at a complete loss to know what to do, and there may be feelings of unreality and of emotional distance from other people. C. S. Lewis can describe his own emotional reactions to his wife's death in the following terms. "There is a sort of invisible blanket between the world and me. I find it hard to take in what anyone says . . . Yet I want others to be about me."[5]

A very opposite symptom may be observed in others, for there is over-activity, approaching frenzy. "O let me not be mad, not mad, sweet heaven! Keep me in temper, I would not be mad" (Shakespeare, *King Lear*, 1.5). Often this loss of control makes the grief all the more painful, and is aptly illustrated in Dostoevsky's *The Brothers Karamazov*. "The sorrow of the common people is ordinarily taciturn and patient, but sometimes it bursts into tears, into lamentation that seems ceaseless, above all those of the women. This sort of grief is no more easy to bear than the silent kind ... it is a dolefulness that does not want consolation: it feeds upon itself."

PSYCHOLOGICAL

1. *Guilt*. When we are stricken by the loss of someone whom we have held dear, the last few weeks or months of the relationship together seem to pass in quick and rapid succession through our minds. The recent past undergoes a keen scrutiny. Trivial incidents of seeming, or actual, neglect, petty quarrels, and misunderstandings which might have occurred are apt to be exaggerated and magnified out of due proportion. The bereaved will tend to think of all the things which might have been done before or during the last illness, or of the different ways in which they might have acted or spoken if only they could have been made aware of what was to happen later.

Miss B had devoted many years to looking after her mother, who had been an invalid. This had entailed constant sacrifice and loss of much social life and contacts on the part of the daughter, who felt keenly this deprivation. Miss B was normally a gay girl, with lots of friends. During the latter stages of Mrs B's illness, there had been times when Miss B unconsciously wished that she might be free from the "tie" and able once again to lead a full life, with some of her evenings free. Outwardly it had been expressed in terms of such expressions as, "O! I do wish Mother would be spared all this suffering." "What a happy release it would be if Mother died quietly in her sleep. ..." After her mother's death she experienced acute guilt feelings, as soon as she felt a sense of relief that she was once more able to lead a normal life.

Mr and Mrs L's son, Ian, had to undergo a heart operation in one of London's teaching hospitals. He was aged six years, and was able to lead a fairly normal life, but unable to join in games and run around much with his school-friends on account of his heart condition. The surgeon had outlined the risks involved in such an operation as his abnormality necessitated, and explained the procedures which it would be necessary to undertake. Unfortunately complications set in after the operation had been carried out, and in the early days of the post-operative stage Ian died. Both parents were completely overcome with a sense of guilt, for they felt entirely responsible for his death after signing the form of consent for the operation to be carried out.

Mr and Mrs M had had a most happy and long married life together, but one morning when Mr M set out for work, they both had cross words over the breakfast table about a trivial incident. On the way to the office Mr M had a coronary thrombosis and was dead on arrival at hospital. Mrs M's grief was uncontrollable, for quite apart from the terrible shock, the words spoken at the breakfast table—the last words they had had together—created much remorse and guilt.

"If only I'd sent for the doctor sooner!", "If only I'd realized that things were going to turn out like this!", and "Why didn't I act sooner, not for one moment did I think he was so ill!" are common expressions of guilt feelings which are commonly heard from the lips of those bereaved. ("Lord, if thou hadst been here, my brother had not died.") The more sensitive the personality, the more marked the sense of guilt. Where there has been actual neglect or indifference, guilt feelings become more marked and severe.

2. *Hostility*. The mourner may resort to feelings of anger and hostility. Both guilt and hostility can result from an attempt to make meaningful, to explain in terms of punishment or sin, the terrible event that has taken place. The idea that death can be an impersonal or accidental event which has no direct reference to the survivor implies a lack of control over the world which most people are not able to accept. The tendency to respond with irritation towards other people is even more marked when those who are nearest

and dearest to the bereaved are present. We could well compare Job's anger towards his friends who were attempting to console him in his troubles. Ina Greer reminds us that "among the early psychoanalysts Freud, Groddeck, and Alexander recognized that the grieving person is somehow an angry person and linked this anger and irritation with the frustration of any close human contact, a frustration and resentment which cannot be expressed because one does not get angry and mistreat one's mother or father, one's child or wife".[6]

If unrecognized, this hostility can quite easily be projected on to others—for example, "Why couldn't the surgeon have saved my boy?" "Why did God allow my son to be taken in this way—so much for your Church and your religion." Where there are bitter self-reproaches a scapegoat has to be found. A typical example is quoted by Howard Becker. A young girl expresses her resentment over her mother's death in the following terms. "There was an old woman about eighty in the hospital where mother was. The very night mother died, this old woman, who was so old that her mind was feeble, sat up in bed and began to whimper. I thought right then that a God that would take my mother, only forty-two years old, and leave that old woman alive, was not a God at all, even if he was [existed]. So I go to church no more."[7]

Unconsciously hostility can be directed towards the deceased, strange as this may appear. "Why have you done this to me, and left me to cope all on my own—what a thing to do!". In her book, *No Longer than a Sigh*, Anne Philipe describes her grief on the death of her young husband Gerard Philipe, the great star of the French theatre and screen. "I must admit that for the first time memories invade me", she confesses. "I call them up, I ask their help to live. I come back to myself and forage in the past. Sometimes I resent you for being dead. You have deserted me, left me. Because of you I can no longer stand grey skies, the rains of November, the last golden leaves, or bare trees I have known with the promise of spring. Once I was light and brave; now I feel heavy, and I drag myself instead of launching into the fray. All is an effort."[8]

Certain grating and irritating features in the relationship of a husband and wife are often recalled, for there are likes and dislikes, disturbing and unpleasant habits in the best and happiest of unions.

Being anxious to combat rather repugnant and ambivalent feelings and to ward off further punishment, there is the tendency to over-emphasize the good qualities and virtues of the deceased. This leads to:

3. *Idealization.* This is demonstrated by such expressions as the following. "He was the ideal husband." "We never had a cross word in all our twenty-two years of married life." Although perhaps not exactly true to real life, such a mechanism can prove an invaluable help in the working through of ambivalent feelings. Idealization is even more marked when bereavement takes place in later life, and can even assume bizarre degrees. With old people there is more opportunity to identify with the deceased rather than feel guilty towards him.[9]

4. *Identification with the deceased.* Another method of dealing with the emotional complications of ambivalence is the adoption of the peculiarities of speech or gesture which were features of the personality of the deceased. This can often be an attempt to carry out the unfulfilled hopes and aspirations of the deceased. "At first, unable to bear even the thought of the everyday occupations and activities that he associates with the lost person, the grief-stricken survivor must concentrate on every object and situation carrying the association until he can accept it emotionally without reawakening his longing."[10]

5. *Preoccupation with the image of the deceased.* So often fantasy occurs and the dead person is seen as though alive again. His presence is felt and his voice distinctly heard, and he may be seen vividly in the dreams of the bereaved.

Lindemann relates how "a patient who lost his daughter in the Coconut Grove disaster visualized his girl in the telephone booth calling for him and was much troubled by the loudness with which his name was called by her, and was so vividly preoccupied with the scene that he became oblivious of his surroundings." Such reactions are also borne out by Marris when he describes the reactions of a young woman in her thirties after the doctor in the hospital had broken the news of her husband's death to her. "I came home", she says, "and, you may not believe me, but I sat down and read the Sunday papers right through, until someone brought me a dinner. I just couldn't realize—not for months. I used to put the kettle on and make tea for him. Or when I'd come home and find him not there, I'd think he'd just gone out— he used to go out a lot in the evenings, not for pleasure but because he had to—and at work, when the girls got talking, I used to think, 'I'll tell Harry that when I get home'." "Altogether", continues Marris, "seventeen mentioned this difficulty in grasping the reality of their husband's death, and fifteen that they continued to behave involuntarily as if he were still alive.... thirty-six had illusions of seeing their husbands, or more often hearing his voice or his footsteps after his death".[11]

Writing on the problems of widowhood, Joan Evelyn[12] can reveal that "while the common-sense of our minds tells us unquestionably that he is *not* there, our emotions and imagination long refuse to believe. Both play tricks with me ... it is no good trying to fight these unreal ideas and thoughts—no good trying to lift your chin up and steel yourself against it. Acceptance of the situation is far better. You *are* like that—your emotions and imagination *do* play tricks with you ..."

Grief can well be compared to an amputation, when a part of oneself has been removed or cut off. As is well known, under such circumstances, so often the organism goes on reacting as if the other member is still there. In the same way a bereaved person has difficulty in accepting the reality of the loss, and fantasy is often preferred to reality. Recalling the death of his twin brother, Noel, in the First World War, Bishop C. M. Chavasse once wrote, "I think my experience has been rather what I went through when I lost my leg. My loss of my twin was like amputation—I felt half of me had gone...I seem still to think over things with Noel, and to feel he might walk into the room any minute..." (*The Chavasse Twins*, Selwyn Gummer, Hodder & Stoughton 1963, pp. 64–5). From a biological standpoint, Darwin pointed out that grief is a conflict between the instinctively based need to cry aloud and search restlessly for the lost object and the learned certainty that such primitive behaviour is fruitless and socially unacceptable. The droop of the mouth and the screwing of the eyes in animals seem to portray an urge to cry, yet at the same time there is the realization of the hopelessness of the situation.

6. *Loneliness, depression, and a feeling of insecurity.* Because of the bereavement, the whole family pattern may be upset. The loved one is now no more, and never again will the family be quite the same, for there is only an aching void which no palliative can remedy.

There will be a strong tendency to shut oneself off from friends. To continue living seems pointless, and the words of St Augustine have a telling ring as he mourns the loss of a friend. "At this grief my heart was utterly darkened", he cried, "and whatever I beheld was death. My native country was a torment to me, and my father's house a strange unhappiness; and whatever I had shared with him, wanting him, became a distracting torture. Mine eyes sought him everywhere, but he was not granted them; and I hated all places, for they had not him...I became a great riddle to myself, and I asked my soul, why she was so sad, and why disquieted me sorely; but she knew not what to answer me... only tears were sweet to me...I was miserable and had lost my joy."[13] Mingled with the depressive state there is a marked inability to sleep and a state of apathy seems to enshroud the sorrowful one.

7. *Anticipatory Grief*. So often during a long, protracted illness, the grief process may have already begun before actual death takes place. The friend or member of family is so preoccupied with his adjustment after the potential death that all the phases of bereavement seems to be experienced—acute preoccupation with the departed, a concern for the various types of death which might befall him, and the consequent readjustments which might have to be made.

We are now in a position to summarize some of the more common reactions to grief as follows:

Physical symptoms:

shock, numbness, sleeplessness, general apathy.

Psychological symptoms:

inability to grasp the situation and comprehend the loss, guilt feelings, resentment and hostility, clinging to the image of the deceased, irritability, and a tendency to isolation.

How long the process of mourning should last is most difficult to clarify. Freud felt that six months would be an approximate duration of time. Lindemann thought that after six weeks there should be signs of recovery, yet Marris found clear evidence of grief persisting for two years after the death of a husband. Probably no mean figure is at all suitable or useful as there is wide variance from person to person. Perhaps all that we can say is that grief seems to reach a peak throughout the second and third weeks and then begins to decline gradually. At anniversaries and birthdays or other reminders of the death it can, however, be revived for years and indeed throughout the remainder of life.

ABNORMAL REACTIONS

Generally speaking abnormal reactions are a result of an exaggeration and/or prolongation of the symptoms described above. They tend to occur when there has been a delay or postponement of grief at the time of death. Latent grief may find expression years afterwards during a later bereavement, when the person might find himself expressing far more sorrow than perhaps the occasion demands or requires—for example, when a mother died there were no tears at all, yet at the death of an aged aunt many years later a great flow of tears and severe grief marked the delayed mourning which previously had gone unexpressed. Linn and Schwarz[14] refer to the autobiographical essay of W. Somerset Maugham (*The Summing Up*) in which he describes how the uncompleted work of mourning over his mother's death affected his grasp of reality. Maugham's mother died when he was eight years of age and he was sent off to a boarding school, and of this period and later he writes thus: "When I was a small boy and unhappy I used to dream night after night that my life at school was all a dream and that I should wake to find myself at home again with my mother. Her death was a wound that fifty years have not entirely healed. I have long ceased to have that dream; but I have never quite lost the sense that my living life was a mirage in which I did this and that because that was how it fell out. . . . When I look back on my life . . . it is shadowy and unsubstantial."

Lindemann classified the various distorted grief reactions as follows:

1. Over-activity without a sense of loss, rather with a sense of well-being and zest, the activities being of an expansive and adventurous nature and bearing semblance to the activities formerly carried out by the deceased.

2. The acquisition of symptoms belonging to the last illness of the deceased. These are often the people who are labelled hypochondriacs or hysterics. The development of symptoms helps the mourner to identify with the deceased, and will often occur during anniversaries or at the age when the deceased himself developed them.

3. A recognized medical disease, namely a group of psycho-somatic conditions, predominantly ulcerative colitis, rheumatoid arthritis, and asthma. The studies in ulcerative colitis revealed that thirty-three out of fifty-one patients developed it in close relationship to the loss of an important person.[15]

4. Alteration in relationship to friends and relatives. All social contact is shunned. So easily can the bereaved live the life of a recluse, avoiding all relationship with others, no matter how eager they are to help.

5. Furious hostility against specific persons. Doctor or surgeon is accused of neglect, and proceedings are often threatened, although rarely carried out.

6. Conduct resembling schizophrenic pictures. These are the people who seem to go about in a continuous daze, behaving in a formal or mechanical way, and to avoid all emotional expression.

7. A complete lack of initiative or drive. The bereaved finds it most difficult to make up his mind or to complete any course of action which is open to him, without the help of friends to advise or even to carry on his life for him.

8. Behaviour which is not in accord with his normal social and economic existence. Unless watched, an abnormally bereaved person will tend to give away large sums of money or enter into financial enactments out of proportion to his income, and without any consideration for the future. The family pattern can become entirely disrupted when such financial speculations are entered upon, and self-punitive behaviour is so marked.

9. Severe depression with insomnia, feelings of utter unworthiness, great tension, bitter self-reproaches, and an obvious need for punishment. When such symptoms are carried to excess there is the tendency to suicide—"Life is just not worth living any more!" "Why go on like this,

when I can end it all?" "I just want to die to be with him!"[16]
It can also lead to psychiatric illness. There is a relatively
high proportion of bereaved among the patients in psychiatric hospitals, and Murray Parkes[17] found that patients who
had lost a spouse shortly before the onset of their mental
illness were five times more frequent among admissions to
the Bethlem Royal and Maudsley Hospitals than would be
expected if the bereavement had not been a cause of the
admission.

The above list of the morbid reactions to bereavement
signify that when grief is either denied or delayed, it can
have devastating effects on those who are in sorrow. However, it must be noted that there are some people who seem
to suffer chronic grief which has neither been delayed nor
denied. These tend to be persons who have always been shy
and timid, tending to invest all their love in one person by
whose loss they are proportionately devastated. Other complicated forms of grief can arise as a result of a relationship
"in which love and hate alternate or negative attitudes have
been repressed. Here the survivor is likely to feel guilty of
having caused the death of the other by the power of his
own wish and he will be deeply disturbed by his guilt."
Again "there is reason to believe from recent studies that
complicated reactions are more likely to occur when the
death has been unexpected and the survivor has had no
time to prepare for it".[18]

Fortunately in the majority of instances the normal reactions are faced courageously and over the months are
eventually worked through successfully. The world begins
to become a less painful place, and the mourner is enabled
to live quite happily and constructively even with the marks
of bereavement within.

4

The Pastoral Care of the Bereaved

Yea, though I walk through the valley of the shadow of death, I will fear no evil; for thou art with me; thy rod and thy staff comfort me. *Ps. 23.4*

We most humbly beseech thee of thy goodness, O Lord, to comfort and succour all them, who in this transitory life are in ... sorrow. *Holy Communion Service, Book of Common Prayer*

This we tell you as the Lord's word; we who are left alive until the Lord comes shall not forestall those who have died ... at the sound of the archangel's voice and God's trumpet-call ... the Christian dead will rise, then we who are left shall join them ... Thus we shall always be with the Lord. Console one another, then, with these words. *1 Thess. 4.15–18 (N.E.B.)*

It is the contagion of our own certainty and faith in immortality that helps most in ministering to those who are bereaved. Many who have themselves endured the pangs of grief and sorrow are of course the more able to enter into fullest sympathy and closest understanding of those who mourn. In offering what help we can at such a time we must remember that those who mourn need understanding of their feelings far more than ready-made solutions to their problems. To "comfort" really means to "strengthen", to "make strong". Mistakenly, it is often understood as a soothing or lulling into forgetfulness. "Should we meet a comforter on the way", warns Emile Cammaerts, "we should make sure that he will not betray us before accepting his company. For the false comforter can only relieve our pain, cover the Cross with flowers, and advise us to wallow in weak apathy or false illusions; but the true Comforter, the giver of strength, touches our shoulders and we stand up; he touches our arm and we pluck the cross from the grave; he touches our foot and we walk carrying the cross on our shoulders; he blesses our pain and it becomes joy, and that blessed joy is as remote from ordinary happiness as that blessed pain from ordinary grief".[1] A sorrowful soul is therefore helped, not so much by hearing words of sympathy to help him forget, but by being strengthened to bear what he has to bear, and to face life again with fresh courage and renewed hope.

PREPARING PEOPLE FOR BEREAVEMENT

If we have been able to establish a good working relationship with the family at the bedside of the dying, then the way is open for further counselling in preparation for the loss when this occurs. Help given at such a time can have a great influence on the way in which they deal with death. We ask ourselves, "Will this family be able to face up to the situation?" "Do I observe signs of panic?" "How much help do I think they will need?" Their actions and words will reveal whether they will be bitter and resentful, or calm and composed. We shall be alert to inter-relationships within the family, and therefore the more able to explore the most helpful avenues of approach.

There will be many conflicting emotions which might prove disturbing to the family, and if they can be anticipated, then the crisis will not be so severe. The majority will need to express their emotions, and they must be prepared and helped to express as much grief as they will feel. They can then be their real selves, rather than suppress their emotions to conform to public convention. Even when the illness has been a lengthy one, the finality of death will still be a shock, and those who have nursed a member of their family over several months will perhaps find it all the more difficult to accept and readjust their lives.

The family might be told that perhaps they will be angry—angry against life in general, or perhaps against God, for such a cruel blow befalling them. C. S. Lewis put into words the doubts of many a mourner, when he confesses,

> Meanwhile, where is God? This is one of the most disquieting symptoms. When you are happy, so happy that you have no sense of needing him. . . . you will be—or so it feels—welcomed with open arms. But go to him when your need is desperate, when all other help is vain, and what do you find? A door slammed in your face, and a sound of bolting on the inside. After that silence . . . Why is he so present a commander in our time of prosperity and so very absent a help in time of trouble? . . . Not that I am (I think) in much danger of ceasing to believe in God. The real danger is of coming to believe such dreadful things about him. The conclusion I dread is not "So there's no God after all", but "So this is what God's really like. Deceive yourself no longer".

In similar circumstances (the death of a wife) the famous preacher, Joseph Parker, had identical sentiments to express,

> In that dark hour I became almost an atheist. How could I be otherwise—my chief joy taken from me—my only joy—the joy that gave gladness to everything else—the joy that made holy work a holy sacrament? O the Gethsemane bitterness! The Calvary solitude! I had secretly prayed God to pity me by sparing her, yet he set his foot upon my prayers, and treated my petitions with contempt. . . . My feet had wellnigh slipped. Then a cruel voice said, "Renounce him! Defy him! He forsook his own Son on the Cross. Hate him, and join us, whom he derides and torments as devils!" My soul was exceeding sorrowful even unto death.

Many will find it difficult to pray and to realize that the Presence of Christ is with them in the very heart of their pain and sorrow. Some will perhaps have doubts about the Love of God and temporarily lose their faith. They can be led to see that this is a phase that will pass when they work through their grief and become strengthened in mind, body, and soul.

We can explain how irritability threatens our relationship with other people at such a time—particularly those who are nearest them, and doing their best to help in the situation. Harsh words might be spoken in the anguish of the moment. It may be hard for them to accept the fact of death, and everything within them will rebel against it. Guilt will be another factor which might be anticipated, so that it might not become morbid, and the bereaved saved from the torments of self-reproach. It can be explained that many a time the mourner will relive the past, and probably be remorseful over seeming neglect or disruptions within the family circle. They will find it difficult to come to terms with reality and will feel dazed and restless, stunned by the element of shock. During sleepless nights innumerable questions will have to remain unanswered. "Ought I to have done more?" "I should have been able in some way to prevent all this happening!" "Have I not failed him in some way?" It is this sense of having "failed" which is particularly hard to bear.

Again the family can be shown that there is present a tendency to exaggerate their own faults and failings and to pass over the weaknesses of others, and so perhaps wish to isolate themselves from other people.

It might be practical to explain *some* of these features, for then grief will be understood, and such reactions seen as normal and natural. Our people will be led to realize what is happening within themselves as they sorrow at the death of a loved one. They will be prepared to recognize their feelings for what they are, and see that they are but passing through the various processes of grief. Such emotions will be seen as in no way unique, or they themselves different from other people who have suffered similarly. Grief that is

understood helps the sorrowful to work through their
bereavement and emerge again step by step to a new life.

GENERAL PRINCIPLES IN COUNSELLING THE BEREAVED

There can be no "stream-line" approach when we minister
to "all them who in this transitory life are in trouble,
sorrow ... or any other adversity". We shall always feel a
great sense of inadequacy, but if we are familiar with some
of the basic elements of bereavement, then we shall understand a little better how those in sorrow feel, and what are
some of the essential factors which help them most at a time
of acute loss and mental anguish. We approach then,
realizing with Oscar Wilde, that "where there is sorrow,
there is holy ground".

By our mere physical presence with a sorrowing family
we shall offer strength and support. Words should always
be kept to a minimum, although one is alway eager to
say something to break a silence which becomes embarrassing to ourselves. How afraid we all are of silence! Helen
Keller once wrote, "'There is little I can say' is often said in
apology by friends. If they but knew that any words—even
the most beautiful—are an intrusion at such a time, and
that the truest sympathy comes with a warm handclasp."

In the initial stage exhortation and advice are not likely
to have any effect on a mind numbed and blunted by an
acute sense of loss. The temptation to prescribe how the
bereaved should feel or react should be avoided at all costs.
They must be left alone to express their feelings in their
own way, and helped to face the reality of what has happened. One of their greatest needs will be to give way to
grief, and nothing we do should hinder or impede such
expression. A further need will be to feel free to recall incidents in the life of the deceased, and here again we can
help them do this, rather than divert the conversation into
other channels or on to other topics. (Is this really done to

help the bereaved, or to create a less threatening situation for ourselves?) "Do tell me more about your husband, Mrs Smith" will encourage many over decisive periods of sorrow. In Hesketh Pearson's *Life of Oscar Wilde* we have a vivid description of how helpful it is to the mourner to talk about the deceased. The account is from "the pen of Mrs H. M. Swanwick" who recalls the following incident.

> When my father died ... my mother nearly went mad with grief. She shut herself up, refusing to see her friends, in a dumb despair. One afternoon Oscar called. I told him of her desperate state, and he said he must see her. She stubbornly refused, and I went back to him to say that I could not prevail on her ... "But she must see me", he replied. "She must. Tell her I shall stay here till she does." Back I went, and for a few minutes my mother sat, crying and wringing her hands, and saying, "I can't. Send him away." Then she arose and went into the room where he was waiting, crying as she went. I saw Oscar take both her hands and draw her to a chair, beside which he set his own; then I left them alone. He stayed a long time, and before he went I heard my mother laughing. When he had gone she was a woman transformed. He had made her talk; had asked questions about my father's last illness, and allowed her to unburden her heart of those torturing memories.

Sympathetic listening will always help to release the grief. If a trustful and meaningful relationship is built up in this way, then those who mourn will be ready to talk and in doing so free themselves gradually from the emotional ties which still bind them to those whom they have loved.

SHOCK AND BEWILDERMENT

At first the bereaved may be inconsolable and completely distraught, physically and emotionally exhausted! It is at this stage that transference can occur, for those who mourn will be in a state of utter dependency. Counter-transference can also arise, and those who minister have to be extremely careful not to become too emotionally involved or overwhelmed with the situation. "No, he's not dead!" "This can't have happened to him!" "Tell me he's alive—it's not real, is it?" Such a state can last for a comparatively short time, yet for some it becomes a protracted phase. When the death is unexpected, these feelings of shock are naturally more intense. Our ministry will not be sufficient if we have merely comforted or consoled. We must proceed to help the sorrowful through the various stages of their reactions, and grief will have to be expressed before help can be effective.

In the early stages our main task will be to listen and help this expression. Urgings to self-control do not penetrate a mind so shocked, and prove psychologically ill advised. Such efforts will only tend to abort the need to cry which at this initial stage is so very necessary.

URGE TO WEEP

It is cathartic to weep, yet we should not attempt to force the bereaved into more expression than they are ready to make at the time. There are some persons who are tearless and mute, and

> Most like a monumental statue set
> In everlasting watch and moveless woe ...
> Touch it; the marble eyelids are not wet.
> If it could weep, it would arise and go.[2]

We learn how to minister from one who himself was "acquainted with grief". When Lazarus, "whom Jesus loved", died, Jesus himself wept (in Moffatt's translation, "he burst into tears"). When Mary learnt that they had taken away her Lord and she knew not where they had laid him, she, too, could not refrain from weeping. Faith does not demand that we maintain a stoical indifference in the face of death. St Ambrose on the death of his brother can write, "We have not incurred any grievous sin by our tears. Not all weeping proceeds from unbelief or weakness. Natural grief is one thing, distrustful sadness is another . . . Tears are marks of devotion, not producers of grief . . . I confess that I too wept, but the Lord also wept. He wept for one not related to him, I for my brother. He wept for all in weeping for one. I will weep for thee in all, my brother." Recalling the tears of Jesus in *A Letter to Mourners*, the late Bishop Bertram Pollock reminds his readers that "He was now identifying himself not only with the sadness of this one scene, but with the grief of all the mourners in all time through the wide world".[3]

Let us do all in our power to help those who remain express as much sorrow as they feel. Liebman reminds us that "we should not grieve when we do not feel it, when, for example, an aged parent who has been suffering from an incurable disease is given surcease by death. On the other hand, we must not be afraid to articulate the wildness of our sorrow if that is what we genuinely feel. We must never falsify our emotions in conformity with conventions . . . after all, we were given tear ducts to use just for such hours of darkness."[4] Never must we insist on a calmness which is either affected or unnatural.

What we must try and help our people avoid, if possible, is the brooding grief which is full of self-pity, for this is the grieving "as those without hope" (1 Thess. 4.13). When Tom Brown visited his old school after hearing of the death of Dr Arnold, he stands reflecting in the school chapel and asks himself, "Am I sorrowing as he would have me sorrow . . . as I should wish to have sorrowed when I shall meet him again?" There is a world of difference between self-pity when thoughts are centred on self, and genuine mourning when hopes and aspirations are centred on God. Little help is promised to the former, for it is only those who *mourn* who will be comforted (Matt. 5.4). "Let us keep hold of our sorrow, never let it leave us . . . only let it be what he would have it—a holy, thankful, cheerful sorrow", wrote Pusey.

The Stoic can never be the ideal example for the Christian in seasons of sorrow and grief. Generally speaking the more easily the bereaved can weep, the more effectively shall we be able to help. When Dicky Vance meets sudden death during the journey *Venture to the Interior*, related by Laurens van der Post,[5] the news has to be broken to Val Vance. Describing this moment, der Post writes, "It was as if I was looking right into a heart suddenly emptied of meaning. I saw something rounded and whole suddenly become such sheer, utter, and black nothingness that my own pulse missed a beat at the horror of it. And then the tears welled up and spilt. I do not know what I should have done if she had not cried. I thanked God for sending those tears so urgently needed, and as I saw her crying bitterly like a child being born, she too seemed to come alive again."

Anxious as we shall be to see evidence of composure as a result of our ministrations, we should never attempt to hurry the whole process of mourning. If we try to short-circuit the emotional processes, we shall only cry "Peace, peace" where there is no peace! Many a sorrowful one would re-echo the words of Marjorie Crosby.

> Nothing in the world can save the reason—remove the hard stone of frozen grief—the wilderness of despair—like tears. Never be afraid to shed them, or to see anyone open the flood gates of her grief. In the cold fear of death—when the fierceness of one's anger has died away—when the fever of jealousy subsides into a dull ache for having spoken unkindly of someone we love—the healing process of tears washes away some of the poison and bitterness. No doctor's medicine—no tender solicitous nursing, no strong tonic, has such a powerful effect on suffering humanity as the shedding of tears. Never be ashamed to shed them; and above all remember that the tears shed for others are precious gifts that are as priceless in God's sight as frankincense and myrrh.[6]

GUILT AND HOSTILITY

In any close relationship guilt and hostility may appear, and after bereavement such feelings have to find expression. Previous to the death they have probably been suppressed.

Constant attempts at further denial will cause delay and interfere with the work of mourning and the effectiveness of our ministry. These can be shown to be but normal forms of grief reaction. "Why did this happen to me?" will be constantly heard as feelings of anger and resentment become part of the process of mourning. If the bereaved express hostility towards the Church or against the seeming cruel Will of God, we must remain calm and unruffled. We shall not agree with what has been expressed, but shall find in the situation a wonderful opportunity of showing the strength of our own faith. It will not be at all helpful to see such an expression as a direct attack, and so respond defensively thus: "O come now, you mustn't say things like that—it's all wrong for you to be thinking this way and you know it!" Such resentment will only prove how threatened we ourselves are, and will form a barrier between the mourner and ourselves, for we shall be quickly seen as "someone who just doesn't understand what it is to feel like this!" Lessons in theology are hardly in place at such a time, for such outbursts are not blasphemies but surely anguished cries of those who are undergoing an intense and bewildering experience. A more helpful reply will be: "I know how you must be feeling at such a time, for it is so hard to accept a sudden loss like this, and it does make us feel hurt and cross. Shall we talk about this together?"

Negative

Positive

In this we do not express or pass judgement on another, neither do we appear shocked at such an insinuation, although not wholly agreeing necessarily with the sentiments expressed. Immediately the sorrowful will sense this understanding and the way is open for further counselling at a later period when some of the initial numbness and bewilderment have worn off.

IDEALIZATION

We have already noted the tendency to extol the virtues of the departed even to the point of incongruity. We must be

ready to accept this, for otherwise the sensitivities of the
bereaved will be needlessly wounded and hurt. At a much
later stage we can help them to gain insight into their
former relationship, shown so clearly in the words of Emile
Cammaerts reflecting over the death of his son. "I should
not, for instance, idealize our past affection in the light of
my present bereavement, and imagine that our love had
reached the perfection which it never reached. We are
divided now, but, in a way, we were always divided. Even
when we were closest together, our souls only groped towards each other in a clumsy and pathetic way. Our communion was never complete because he remained himself,
and I remained myself, and because between father and son,
indeed between husband and wife, there always are some
obstacles which cannot be completely overcome ..."[7]

Idealization can at the time be one of the simplest ways
of resolving guilt feelings, and plays a major part in the
Jewish methods of mourning.[8] "On returning from the
burial, 'shiva' commences—the seven days during which
the mourner is confined to the house in which he sits on
the floor or on a low bench, devoting his time to the reading
of the book of Job. The first meal after the funeral is prepared by a neighbour and is called 'the meal of consolation'. Friends and neighbours come to visit the mourner,
and the conversation is limited to *the praises of the deceased*".[9]

PREOCCUPATION WITH THE DECEASED

It is essential that the family be as emancipated as possible
from the deceased. Although the physical presence of the
loved one has been withdrawn "many of the psychological
ties still exist, and as they exist, the bereaved cannot be free
to rebuild his life. The acuteness of the need depends upon
the meaning which the deceased had for the bereaved. The
greater the importance of the rôle which the deceased had
played for the bereaved, the greater need the latter has for

being given an opportunity to free himself from him ... For a man who found his wife not only a partner, but a mother-substitute as well, there will be greater loss when she dies than there would be for another who was psychologically weaned from his mother before his marriage took place."[10]

We should therefore always try to help our people face their loss, painful as this will be for them. Otherwise frustration will result and they will become more and more depressed. Acceptance of the situation as it is is far more helpful, and we must assist in this process as discreetly and wisely as we can.

LONELINESS AND DEPRESSION

What we are will matter far more than what we attempt to say no matter how beautifully expressed our words might be. With humility and utter sincerity we shall have to confess that we cannot answer all the questions asked. We do not pretend to be able to understand or interpret what the Will of God might be. It is not given to man to know all the mysteries of pain and sadness. Rather confess our very stumblings and gropings than utter pious clichés which mean so very little. Our conversation will be directed towards the emotional needs of our people, and as they repeat the story of the death over and over again and the incidents which led up to it we follow with patience and sympathy. We shall *explore* rather than *exhort*. We help but little in such sayings as "It's a blessing!" "A happy release!" "Better this than ———". "Time will heal ..." "People bring us but miserable consolation when they tell what time will do to help our grief," writes Bishop Phillips Brooks, "because our grief is bound up with our love and we could not cease to mourn without being robbed of our affections ... Let me remember for ever, even if everlasting memory means everlasting pain. You add a new pang to my sorrow when you tell me that some day I shall escape it by forgetfulness."

Let us avoid, too, the attempt to comfort by "reminding our people that death is a common experience and that in six months they will feel differently. For all the common-ness, theirs is a unique experience, and for all the healing power of time, not to grieve now would be to lose all too quickly the love which bound the union. To encourage cheerfulness too soon is to create a feeling of faithlessness to the departed, and to increase their anguish. To offer the assurance of eternal life prematurely is to fail to recognize the factor of absence and separation which, in spite of one's belief in immortality, is very real."[11] Carroll Wise (Pastoral Counseling, Its Theory and Practice: Harper: N.Y. 1951, p. 215) emphasizes how "premature urging of the idea of immortality may retard the emotional readjustment to be-reavement" by quoting a mother, mourning her son. "The more she thought about the son being 'up in heaven' the more she suffered because he was not here on earth." If the bereaved are to be helped to express as much grief as they feel, they will not be helped by coercion to adopt a "stiff-upper-lip" attitude, with exhortations of, "You mustn't cry." "Do be brave." "He/She wouldn't want you to cry like this." "Please! —you mustn't show the others you've been crying!"

In his *Letters to Malcolm* (Letter 8, pp. 6off), C. S. Lewis shows how strong "the temptation is to attempt reassur-ances", and how "even now certain remembered moments of fallacious comfort twist my heart more than the re-membered moment of despair.... Far from lightening the dark valley where you now find yourself, I blacken it ... I think it is only in shared darkness that you and I can really meet at present; shared with one another and, what matters most with our Master. We are not on an untrodden path. Rather, on the main road." Instead of helping the bereaved to get *over* their sorrow, it is sometimes ours to help them get *into* it, provided of course that we go down *with them* into the valley of the shadow.

In our ministry we have to have clear in our minds two different types of depression. As this is most difficult and only clear to the most experienced, some words of Sullivan may help us.

> There is just about as much difference between sadness and depression as there is between any two things that pertain to people, but the initial impression does not clearly differentiate them. Depressed people look and sound sad; and if a person looks and sounds sad, the perceived state is that of sadness. Whether the apparent sadness is a sign of depression—which is a very much more serious and quite different state—will gradually become evident. Sorrow can always be explained. That is, if the person feels willing and free to tell the interviewer what he feels grieved by, the account will be meaningful ... but the depressed person's explanation for his sadness ... puts him in a class with all the great martyrs of history ...[12]

There will be need to set a limit to mourning. Gorer has shown the confusion existing among people as to how long they should grieve, and shows us that perpetual grief is not rare. Often the termination of the ritual of mourning can help bring to an end the inner state of which this is an expression. Marris also explains that "since the conventional length of mourning is so ill defined, a widow stands in all the more need of reassurance that her grief has sincerely shown her love, and the time has come to be reconciled. Besides friends and relatives, people in positions of moral authority, such as doctors or ministers of religion, can sometimes help to give this sanction, because their position gives weight to their judgement and endorses the soundness of their advice". Several of the widows interviewed by Marris mentioned "that they had begun to pull themselves together after a remark which they accepted as a sign to leave off grieving". When such advice has to be given let it be done with as much discretion and feeling as possible.

THE DOCTOR AND NURSE

Let both doctor and nurse deal very gently and patiently with all who are in sorrow, and try to understand what the separation means to the family concerned. They will have to watch their own feelings, for anxiety and insecurity can quickly be transferred to those who are in distress of mind. They will help but little if they themselves are too upset or emotionally involved. At the same time it is necessary "for the physician to give the patient the full measure of his emotional support and sympathy in bearing the pain of this process (i.e. bereavement) and for him to mobilize other sources of support within the family and outside it. In this regard the physician should realize that emotional support depends, among other factors, on the quantity of personal interaction, so he should realize the special importance of even short extra visits to his patient during the mourning period, or, if these are not possible under the pressure of a busy practice, at least of telephone communication. Since the pathological sequels of inadequate mourning are usually so severe, these extra visits are well worth while", writes Gerald Caplan.[13]

It will often fall within the nurse's duty to inform the next of kin of the death of a patient. Such news is always best communicated to the family group rather than to individuals. This, of course, will be done in a most discreet and tactful manner, and if the nurse has been able to anticipate some of the reactions of the family under such circumstances so much the better. Opportunities to discuss their whole ministry to the bereaved should be given to all nurses during their periods of block-training.

With a watchful and perceptive mind comes the ability to glean a little of the feelings which the bereaved express, and to respond accordingly. Sedatives have a place in excessive grief or when the family show extreme exhaustion, but they can sometimes be far too readily given and blunt the edge of a grief which is longing to find expression at a critical stage. By such means the doctor or nurse can bring relief both to the bereaved—and to themselves!—but the basic problem still exists and remains untouched.

The nurse can be assured that those in sorrow are "never

likely to forget their hours around the bed of the loved one
who had died; over and over again they will recount everything that has happened ... they will always bring some
reference to the kindness and sympathy of the nurse who
was there and how much she helped to ease the burden of
their pain ... the records of the hospital may show her to
have been a nurse who gained no particular distinction but,
in the grateful hearts of common men and women, she will
be a most gracious memory".[14]

When the first pangs of grief are over, the Christian
doctor and nurse can play their part as members of the
Body of Christ. They can "comfort all who mourn" with a
suitable prayer for the departed and for those who mourn.
If the hospital chaplain or local priest has not already
seen the family, he can be sent for to offer all the help that
only the Church can bring by prayer and sacrament. If
death takes place in the hospital, and the visitors' room is
situated near, those who sorrow can be taken to the hospital
chapel for quiet meditation and spiritual rest, should they
so wish.

THE SOCIAL WORKER

In the interviews that the social worker will have with the
bereaved, it is most helpful to recount some of the episodes
of the family prior to the death, for as a result of such discussions together she will be able to form a picture of the
various relationships within the family unit. In this way
the social worker will then assess and understand a little
more clearly what the bereavement has really meant to
those who are intimately and personally involved. During
these talks "the little things we used to do together" will be
remembered and recounted.

In the interviews, after idealization has been expressed,
the social worker will often be alert for some of the more
negative attitudes of hostility to be indirectly implied—for
example, "Sometimes she used to get very irritable—and
life was not all honey very often!" "We used to have our

quarrels you know—it's only natural, isn't it?" If such remarks are forthcoming, let there be no urge or hurry to explain or interpret. The social worker will find it far more helpful to try to clarify the position by saying, "When did these quarrels occur, Mrs B?" or "Please do tell me a little more about some of the times when you were irritable, Mr C." "What happened usually on these occasions?" "Did they occur very frequently, as far as you can recall?" "Do let me hear exactly how you felt about things." "Do you find it very hard to express what you really felt at the time?" "Why should this be, I wonder?" "Do you think you can tell me some of the reasons why you reacted as you did at the time—how you really felt?" To express themselves adequately does not come easily, and gradually the social worker may continue, "Did you feel really cross and annoyed with Mr B sometimes?" "Why do you think you found it hard to express your feelings at the time ... ?" If the social worker helps the bereaved to see that sometimes it is but natural for people to feel bitter or hostile or angry under certain circumstances, she has indeed helped much.

In an interview conducted in this manner with discretion, the mourner is helped to talk and release his emotions, and so successfully work through the various stages of his grief in a warm, receptive, and sympathetic atmosphere. The social worker will have shown him that she really understands and realizes what the loss has involved in family relationships. She can now help him to face the future, finding satisfaction in new relationships. He can be linked to a church with its organizations and fellowship, and led to a new meaning to life. The family as a unit can thus be helped to ascend the mount of sorrow and grief and descend once more into the plain of inner peace and security.

THE FRIEND OR RELATIVE

When a person has been smitten with grief it is difficult for him to function normally. He will want to talk rather incessantly and the relative or friend must exercise the greatest patience. He will feel insecure, and to have the family around him will encourage and support him, for it will mean the world to have about him those who really understand and know the family situation, and what the death has really involved of pain and perhaps hardship. However, we have already seen how small irritations can grate at such a time and words be spoken harshly to those who are attempting to be of the greatest help. Indeed it may be true to say that there are more family upsets and quarrels as a result of things said during bereavement than in any other situation. Friends and neighbours are apt to take offence on such occasions—"Fancy her saying that after all I've done for her. I'll never go near the house again!"—rather than understand that such remarks are but the natural outcome of a bewildering situation.

It is not always wise to persuade the bereaved person to "go off for a change" (unless of course his health demands it) if the real intention is to escape from things, for the facing of the inevitable on return will be the more difficult. One of the most helpful duties of friends and relatives will be to see that he is kept in contact with the world at large, and that he does not retreat within himself. He can be encouraged to renew social contacts and perhaps cultivate new interests.

Again, let there be a period of thought and consideration before "snap decisions" are taken, for it will prove more beneficial to move slowly and give much forethought to future plans. Friends, however, must not take over control of the situation and make decisions, but be ready at the side to guide and advise.

Visits should be regularly arranged to the home, especially over birthdays and anniversaries, for these are times when the bereaved will feel their loss most keenly, and if they pass forgotten a sense of utter desertion and abandonment will ensue. Such calls are of paramount importance during the weeks or months after the funeral, and availability and readiness to help are the two most important factors involved. The work of consolation is indeed most difficult, for "sympathy may only aggravate distress: exhortations to be practical and look to the future seem glib and insensitive, solicitousness seems officious—the comforters seem to fuss ineffectually outside a conflict that they cannot understand, when all she (i.e. the widow) wants is to be left alone. They can best guide her recovery by encouraging her patiently to feel that she has mourned enough."[15]

THE PRIEST

It is the priest who has meditated upon death and understood some of the spiritual and psychological problems relating to grief and bereavement who can best help and inspire those in sorrow. In his anxiety to help, he must be careful not to blur the physical reality of the dead with *premature* spiritual reassurances. To try to bolster up a spirit of hopefulness with excessive religious affirmations too early after the shock of a death can create thoughts of faithlessness and increase feelings of guilt.

In the initial stage he will "stand or sit quietly by silently praying may be, but with poise and calm, saying by his presence that he does understand and that he is there to give support". He will "study to be quiet", or rather in the words of the *N.E.B.* "let it be [his] desire to keep calm". In this way a real spirit of empathy is instilled and a meaningful dialogue takes place. Empathy then becomes "an active process of being there—to be able to go where the sufferer wants to go, to be able by standing there to communicate *I understand*, without saying so in so many words ... practising the presence of quietness in bearing and attitude creates the atmosphere in which another can begin to unburden himself".[16]

The priest must be specially careful not to imply that the expression of grief betrays a lack of faith in the doctrine of the Resurrection. Surely we should be less than human, not more than human if we never wept at the loss of someone very dear to us. "We must not premeditate too much", wrote Vinet over a hundred years ago, "what we shall say or what we shall do on these occasions. The best meditation is thinking of their misfortunes, the best preparation is a sincere and abundant pity ... let us go with God himself, with the certainty that he will be with us and with them."[17]

By his permissive attitude, the priest opens the way for the bereaved to feel perfectly free to discuss their fears, their resentments, and their doubts, and so be more and more aware of the love and mercy of God toward them. He will "encourage recollections and reveal a boundless patience in listening to the bereaved. He should not cut short the stories or be annoyed by endless repetitions. He has to understand that grief work must come from within and be done by the bereaved himself. There are no short cuts to the inner growth and maturation of a person, but wise guidance may help the bereaved to gain a new horizon and to see past events in a new perspective."[18]

When such remarks as "I'm so sorry to hear of your trouble, Mrs S, but I know you'll be brave and have faith for the sake of the others" are made, they subtly tend to suppress and delay the act of mourning. They imply that at all costs the bereaved must not show their grief, and that their faith should be adequate to meet the situation in this stoical manner. A greater sense of guilt is thus instilled, and should they "break down", what faith they had suffers a bitter blow. Probably far more helpful are statements such as, "I'm so very sorry to hear of the death of Mr G. You may be assured that we all realize a little how you must be feeling at this time, for we know how much you will miss your husband, Mrs G." or, "I shall be pleased to do all I possibly can to help you *face* this sad bereavement ..."

If the priest points out how the bereaved should be acting under the circumstances, feelings of guilt will be increased when these expectations and exhortations fail to be fulfilled. The mourner will be eager to say what he feels the priest would want him to say, rather than give vent to his real feelings and reactions. "Rule of thumb approaches are out of place", warns C. Murray Parkes, "and the handling of a bereavement must be based upon a knowledge of the particular circumstances. It is easy for the well-meaning helpers to rush in and force the bereaved person to face facts, give up his defences, and break down. Such a frontal assault may well result in severe depression or an aggressive refusal of further help. At the other extreme is the over-tactful sympathizer who, by encouraging defence (for instance by refusing to discuss the death or deifying the dead), only perpetuates the reaction. Useful help would seem to lie somewhere between these two extremes."[19]

Although he may be aware of both the psychological and physical reactions to bereavement, it is not his task in his pastoral care to probe deeply for feelings of hostility or guilt. Rather is it essential for him to understand some of the more common factors in order to minister more effectively to his people in sorrow and grief. He will consequently be the more able to establish a meaningful relationship (rapport) which is the first essential for his counselling work. The warmth of his concern and the depth of his acceptance help the parishioner to express his emotional tensions and so gain insight and perspective which are so very necessary to work through his grief. If there has been real guilt or neglect, then the parishioner can be led to Confession and Absolution and thus gain peace of mind and soul. This can also be an opportunity for his spiritual life to be strengthened and deepened, and the future faced with a clearer knowledge of Christian Death and Resurrection.

One of the great practical difficulties facing the priest is the burial of people whom he has never met before, and about whose families he knows very little or nothing at all. This is further aggravated by the procedures of "cemetery/crematorium rota" which occurs regularly in some areas, and involves the priest in officiating over a series of burials or cremations in fairly quick succession. Under such conditions as these, he cannot possibly be aware of the needs of each family concerned. In many instances he will not even be aware of more than their names. Neither can he possibly be fully sensitive or sympathetic toward them when burial follows burial, and family follows family. Such funerals may prove far too numerous for him to follow up even when they reside in his parish, or to refer them to their respective priests and ministers when they live elsewhere. He can be helped, however, on these occasions by the funeral director[20] who can at least tell him a few facts about the death and the reactions of the family concerned, so that when time allows he can express his concern for their strain and stress. In this way many an opportunity for evangelism can be fostered whenever there can be a visit to the home, and perhaps result in leading a family back into the fold of the Church because of what was said at the time of trouble.

Finally, the priest will be alert to note any signs or symptoms of abnormal grief. Since the difference between the normal and abnormal is a matter of line drawing rather than an easy decision, we can only draw attention to particular danger signs:

1. When the symptoms of grief become severe and prolonged, and the priest begins to feel, "I don't quite understand what is happening here—things should be definitely improving by this time—there are factors at work which are beyond me."

2. When a marked change in the behaviour-pattern is evident. A socially well-adapted person becomes shut in and completely introverted, with no desire at all to return to former activities even after a prolonged period of grief.

3. When depression becomes overwhelming and all self-esteem seems to be lost. This may be coupled with a threat of suicide, and all such threats have to be taken seriously. "I just want to die and be with him." "Death is the only thing left now!"

4. When a marked sense of hostility shows no signs of lessening, and resentment towards others increases with a general suspicion of everyone.

5. When there are obvious signs of hallucinations (to be distinguished from the fantasies which have a part in normal grief), or symptoms indicative of mental disorder—for example, loss of contact with reality.

6. A complete denial that death has taken place. The bedroom is kept exactly as it was at the time of death; the table still laid with a place reserved for the deceased, and the home set in readiness for his return one day.

7. When the bereaved become mute and regressed over a long period of time, with a complete failure to break away from fixed patterns. An aimlessness and inability to relate to the present situation.

8. When there are signs of manic-depressive reaction. There will perhaps be a false sense of elation alternating with depression and a withdrawal from all sense of responsibility.

9. A continual state of panic which all reassurance and counselling have failed to assuage.

10. When a widow or widower seeks to assuage grief in alcoholism.

Many will have probably been people who have been deeply disturbed from time to time before bereavement took place, and whose grief has now accentuated their troubles. When such symptoms are perceived by the priest, he will do well to refer them to the general practitioner concerned, or through him to a psychiatrist. In no case should he attempt to shoulder these difficulties *alone*, for they need medical and psychiatric help. This will in no way signify desertion, for he will still have them under his pastoral care, and they will look to him for spiritual guidance rather than for psychiatric attention. With the various sources of help available working and ministering *together* in closest co-operation and good will, the bereaved parishioner will be helped to face the future with increased hope and inner stability.

5

Facing the Future

We owe it to the dead ... not to let ourselves be
crushed; saddened we must be ... but not broken,
not weaker, or less resolute to fight out to the end
what is truly the Battle of Life. LORD MILNER

You do not understand now what I am doing, but
one day you will.   *John 13.7 (N.E.B.)*

And when the strife is fierce, the warfare long,
Steals on the ear the distant triumph song,
And hearts are brave again, and arms are strong.
                    WILLIAM WALSHAM HOW

It is when the funeral is over and friends have left that the
priest's ministry can perhaps be most effective, especially if
a good working relationship has already been established.
The bereaved are now left on their own to cope with their
affairs and to make the necessary readjustments for the
future. In his first post-funeral visit the priest may feel that
everything appears reasonably well; the widow/widower has
taken it all so courageously, and there is probably no further
need for him to follow up his pastoral calling. So often such
a situation can prove most deceptive. Under the façade of
outward courage and fortitude there can lurk many fears
and frustrations longing to find expression. Rather than a
"good sign", the very opposite can sometimes be true, and
the wise priest must be on the alert for this.

The critical time will probably last for some two or three
months, and contact should be kept with the family throughout this important phase of mourning. Regular visits should

be paid over the weeks, and if the priest can arrange to be present when anniversaries of the death occur his ministry will be much appreciated.

Many who mourn are most anxious to busy themselves as much as they possibly can, and they enter upon a state of frenzied activity. It is of course good to be "up and doing", but if this activity is merely an attempt to "forget about things" or "push things on one side", it cannot be as therapeutic as it might be. To shut off all thoughts of the loss incurred will only serve to delay outlet and expression until a later time. Another tendency will be to withdraw from social contacts and activities, as has already been noted. This might be coupled with the thought that no form of enjoyment should be entered upon again, or that in some strange sense one ought not to be feeling happier. "There's no denying that in some sense I 'feel better'," writes C. S. Lewis, "and with that comes at once a sort of shame, and a feeling that one is under a sort of obligation to cherish and foment and prolong one's unhappiness. I've read about that in books, but I never dreamed I should feel it myself. I am sure H wouldn't approve of it. She'd tell me not to be a fool. So, I'm pretty certain, would God."[1]

Life without friends will always prove most lonely and frustrating, for their presence and their prayers will help much. In one of his Essays—"On Friendship"—Bacon wrote that "friendship works two contrary effects, for it redoubleth joys and cutteth griefs in half". Joshua Liebman in *Peace of Mind* puts it like this. "The melody that the loved one played upon the piano of your life will never be quite the same again, but we must not close the keyboard and allow the instrument to gather dust. We must seek out other artists of the spirit, new friends who will gradually help us to find the road to life again, who will walk that road with us."

Now is the time to interest the bereaved in a cause for which they can work, or interests and hobbies which they can develop. In this way, new contacts are made and fresh vistas opened.

I was in the depths of grief, I might also say of despair, [wrote John Bright] for all the light and sunshine of my house had been extinguished. All that was left on earth of my young wife, except the memory of a sainted life and of a brief happiness, was lying still and cold in the chamber above us. Mr Cobden called upon me as a friend, and addressed me, as you might suppose, with words of condolence. After a time he looked up and said: "There are thousands of houses in England at this moment where wives, mothers, and children are dying of hunger, hunger made by the laws. Now", he said, "when the first paroxysm of your grief is passed, come with me, and we will never rest till those laws are repealed." I accepted his invitation.

By the grace of God, it is always amazing what strength is granted at a time of deep sorrow, when the darkness of the valley of the shadow envelops the soul. Often we shall be forced to say: "I just don't know where I had the strength from!" "If someone could have shown me what I would have to go through, I just wouldn't have believed it possible!" Much will depend upon our own efforts, for bereavement is very much what we make of it, but "if we are honest, and trace the trail still further back, we shall realize that God has poured in fresh supplies to reinforce our short resources of faith and courage. One of the things we learn through grief is a greater capacity for drawing on the love and peace and strength of God."[2]

In James Agee's prize-winning novel called *A Death in the Family*, Mary, whose husband has been tragically killed, is able to reflect on her experience of bereavement and say, "'I am carrying a heavier weight that I could have dreamed it possible for a human being to carry, yet I am living through it'... She thought that she had never before had the chance to realize the strength that human beings have to endure; she loved and revered all those who had ever suffered ... she thought that she had never before had the chance to realize the might, grimness, and tenderness of God. She thought that now for the first time she began to know herself, and she gained extraordinary hope in this beginning of knowledge. . . ."

With a more mature faith and a more hopeful outlook those who sorrow can possess an inner tranquillity which infuses them with new and unexpected strength. It is belief in "the Communion of Saints, the resurrection of the body, and the life everlasting" that becomes the one most effective instrument of healing. The reading of the Scriptures, particularly the Gospel stories, will bring much comfort. The life, death, and resurrection of our Lord will enable faith to remain solid and steadfast. The priest can guide his people to selected passages where he who reads will learn afresh of the nearness of God and his love and concern for those who mourn. The bereaved will pray for their faithful departed. "Eternal rest grant them, O Lord, and let light perpetual shine upon them." We pray that they may be given "the rest which is full of change, yet ever the same; the rest of those of whom it is written: They rest not day nor night from his perfect service". We ask that light may be granted them—"not fitful light, gleams coming and going, discoveries vanishing in the light of new discoveries, light succeeded by spells of darkness and ignorance; but 'light perpetual', steady, persistent, 'shining more and more unto the perfect Day'."[3]

In the Sacrament of the Altar "we offer this sacrifice in memory of all those who are fallen asleep before us" (St Cyril of Jerusalem) as "we bless thy holy name for all thy servants departed this life in thy faith and fear; beseeching thee to give us grace to follow their good examples, that with them we may be partakers of thy heavenly kingdom". We recall St Monica's dying wish to her son St Augustine: "Lay this body anywhere; let not the care for that disquiet you in any way. The one thing I ask of you is, that you will remember me at the altar of the Lord."[4]

If we live in this faith then we shall be able to agree with those wonderful words of Dean Inge, himself languishing in deep sorrow over the death of his small daughter.

> Bereavement is the deepest initiation into the mysteries of human life, an initiation more searching and profound than even happy love. Love remembered and consecrated by grief belongs, more clearly than the happy intercourse of friends, to the eternal world; it has proved itself stronger than death. Bereavement is the sharpest challenge to our trust in God; if faith can overcome this, there is no mountain which it cannot remove. And faith can overcome it. It brings the eternal world nearer to us, and makes it seem more real. It is not that we look forward to anything remotely resembling Ezekiel's vision of the valley of the dry bones. Still less could we find any comfort from the pathetic illusions of modern necromancy. These fancies have nothing to do with our hope of immortality, which would be in no way strengthened by such support. Rather does pure affection, so remembered and so consecrated, carry us beyond the bourne of time and place altogether. It transports us into a purer air, where all that has been, is, and will be lives together, in its true being, meaning and value before the throne of God.[5]

"How blest are the sorrowful: they shall find consolation" (Matt. 5.4, *N.E.B.*).

PART TWO

The Funeral

But the greatest thing of all other about this duty of Christian burial is an outward testification of the hope which we have touching the resurrection of the dead. For which purpose let any man of reasonable judgement examine, whether it be more convenient for a company of men as it were in a dumb show to bring a corpse to the place of burial, there to leave it covered with earth, and so end, or else to have the exequies devoutly performed with solemn recital of such lectures, psalms and prayers, as are purposely framed for the stirring up of men's minds unto a careful consideration of their estate both here and here-after.

RICHARD HOOKER

O merciful God, the Father of our Lord Jesus Christ, who is the resurrection and the life; in whom whosoever believeth shall live, though he die; and whosoever liveth, and believeth in him, shall not die eternally; who also hath taught us (by his holy Apostle Saint Paul) not to be sorry as men without hope, for them that sleep in him: We meekly beseech thee, O Father, to raise us from the death of sin unto the life of righteousness; that, when we shall depart this life, we may rest in him, as our hope is this our *brother* doth; and that, at the general Resurrection in the last day, we may be found acceptable in thy sight, and receive that blessing which thy well-beloved Son shall then pronounce to all that love and fear thee, saying, Come, ye blessed children of my Father, receive the kingdom prepared for you from the beginning of the world: Grant this, we beseech thee, O merciful Father, through Jesus Christ, our Mediator and Redeemer. *Amen.*

Prayer Book Collect: At the Burial of the Dead.

But, you may ask, how are the dead raised? In what kind of body? A senseless question! The seed you sow does not come to life unless it has first died; and what you sow is not the body that shall be, but a naked grain, perhaps of wheat, or of some other kind; and God clothes it with the body of his choice, each seed with its own particular body. All flesh is not the same flesh: there is flesh of men, flesh of beasts, of birds, and of fishes—all different. There are heavenly bodies and earthly bodies; and the splendour of the heavenly bodies is one thing, the splendour of the earthly, another. The sun has a splendour of its own, the moon another splendour, and the stars another, for star differs from star in brightness. So it is with the resurrection of the dead. What is sown in the earth as a perishable thing is raised imperishable. Sown in humiliation, it is raised in glory; sown in weakness, it is raised in power; sown as an animal body, it is raised as a spiritual body.

1 Cor. 15.35–44 (N.E.B.)

Among Christians the honour which is valued in the behalf of the dead is, that they be buried in holy ground; that is, in appointed cemeteries in places of religion, there where the field of God is sown with the seeds of the resurrection, that their bodies also may be among the Christians.   JEREMY TAYLOR

The function of
the Funeral Director and information
useful for the Priest

The function of a funeral director is to be technical adviser, agent, contractor, master of ceremonies, and custodian of the body for his client.

In the first place, the client is apt to think in terms of employing a funeral contractor, in other words an undertaker. Almost inevitably he finds himself using the funeral director as technical adviser, appealing to him as an expert and often as an experienced, sympathetic listener and confidant.

It is the funeral director's duty to provide all the necessary information of available choices, rights, unavoidable duties, and the manner of their performance; to give or to obtain answers to any queries whatsoever that may arise, to accept instructions for the carrying out of any lawful wish that may be expressed, however unfamiliar and however contrary to his own preferences, beliefs, or prejudices.

The funeral director should study to achieve a manner and a type of ceremony which will express the style of his client as he understands it, without the client having expressed any wishes. The funeral director who fails to do this will be capable of carrying out funerals only to the satisfaction of people of his own limited kind.

It is his duty in every eventuality to suggest from his own experience the most effective way in which to express the ideas of his client. He is also responsible for the fulfilment of his instructions in every detail to the limit of possibility and legality. He must at all times regard as confidential all instructions, confidences, or casually gained information concerning a client's affairs. A very important duty is to advise on the scale of spending in the best interest of a client at a time when he is emotionally most susceptible to extravagance.

He must be prepared to take the body of the deceased person into his charge and care, a duty which is the very core of the funeral director's responsibility to his client, handling and housing it with both care and respect for the dignity of the deceased. Preservative treatment (embalming) and the prevention of shocking visual memories are a duty to his client.

To the public and to the authorities, the funeral director owes a responsible approach to infectious diseases and to insanitary conditions of any sort arising from death.

The funeral director has also, of course, yet another responsibility—that to his professional colleagues. He must behave with such dignity and propriety and especially speak of his work at all times in such a way that he upholds the reputation and status of funeral directors in general in the eyes of the public. He will not advertise anything that will offend against good taste. The code of conduct of the National Association of Funeral Directors should be noted in these respects.

He should use his Local Association to obtain the fullest amenities that his clients need. The Association can, and does, approach crematoria, cemeteries, mortuaries, registrars, local government officers, and police on various issues. Use of this service is not just a privilege of membership of the National Association of Funeral Directors, but also a definite duty to the public.

INTERVIEW WITH FAMILY

The "arrangements" interview is a sort of planning conference with the emphasis upon the desires of the relatives of the deceased. The wishes of the client are paramount, and the funeral director is present to lend his specialized knowledge and experience in converting the client's desires into a carefully arranged plan.

If the interview is at the office, provision should be made for the discussions to be in private. If in the home, the funeral director must needs adapt himself to the family circle.

The first rule for all such interviews is—*not to hurry*. Remember that this is the only funeral the relatives are interested in. They must get the impression that the funeral director's one object is to serve them; he should, therefore, take his time.

If the client is disposed to talk, let him do so, a few minutes spent in friendly conversation is time well spent. It helps to get to know the clients and in the process it eases the tension and helps them to relax. The funeral director should be a good listener and let them talk. In this way, he will soon have a general picture of their wishes for the arrangements. At least the funeral director should have ascertained whether it is to be cremation or earth burial.

Now the funeral director is in a position to get out his instruction card and note down the essential information. Answers to questions should still be obtained by using a conversational approach. The interview must in no way resemble a third degree examination or the completing of a government form. It is an intimate family affair, and the funeral director's attitude must be that of a friendly adviser.

Nevertheless, it is important that full details be obtained, and in this respect the instruction sheet or card is a vital document. The National Association has given intensive study to perfecting forms for this purpose and now publishes three types of forms: (*a*) a form specifically for burial arrangements; (*b*) a form designed for cremation arrangements; (*c*) a combined form for either burial or cremation. These forms set out all the information required. Therefore, this card, used throughout by the funeral director, ultimately becomes a complete record of the funeral, from which the office extracts all the information required.

CLERGY AND SERVICE

When a family attend church, they usually desire the services of their own minister. Yet it is remarkable how often it occurs that they will name their church and yet not know the minister's name. Therefore, a knowledge of the local clergy is a great asset and the funeral director's ability to supply the information wins the approval of the client.

The funeral director should offer to make all arrangements with the clergy. Even if the family wish to speak to their minister personally, it is still advisable to have their permission for him to fix the details as to time and also to arrange transport for the minister (if this is necessary).

The funeral director must have knowledge of the requirements of different denominations. He is also well advised to make a note of the names of individual clergy in his locality.

As to the actual service, the alternatives for the family to consider are: in the church, in the home, in the private chapel, at the cemetery or the crematorium.

When a family are regular church attenders, it is certainly good practice to suggest that the Service be held in their own church. This is appreciated by the family and the clergy. The funeral director needs to inquire whether music is desired and, if so, to ask if they have any requests for favourite hymns. At this stage, it might be suggested that specially printed service sheets be provided, in which case the minister must be consulted as to the order of the service.

When a service in the home is requested the funeral director needs to know the feeling of the local clergy in this respect. With all Free Church denominations there is no objection. The Church of England and the Roman Catholics in most dioceses insist that the service be in the parish church or cemetery chapel, or, in the case of the Church of England only (as Roman Catholics do not accept cremation) in a crematorium chapel; but in all cases it is usually possible to arrange for family prayers in the home.

Generally speaking, the attitude of the clergy towards services in private chapels at the funeral director's premises is as stated in respect of services in the home. Personal contacts and friendly co-operation with the clergy is of mutual benefit to all concerned.

There are many families who have little or no connection with any particular Church. In most cases they claim allegiance to one or other denomination. In such cases, the local knowledge of the funeral director is very helpful. He should first suggest that he arrange with the minister of the parish in the case of the Church of England or with the nearest minister of any Free Church denomination they name. Usually, the minister appreciates such an introduction to the family.

Very often the minister is placed in a very difficult position owing to his lack of knowledge of the family, and it is here that the funeral director can (without breaking any confidence) help by supplying such general background information that he may have gained while making the funeral arrangements, i.e. relationship of the principal mourner—if the death is a normal one (after illness), or the result of an accident, etc., and when (as is often the case) the surviving spouse goes to stay with a son or daughter or other relative and the house is shut up, he can be given this address and thus be saved a fruitless visit to an empty house. This small service is much appreciated by the clergy and builds goodwill.

There is also the alternative available in most fair-sized towns, namely a rota of cemetery duty, arranged by the clergy in conjunction with the Cemetery or Crematorium Authority.

PRESS NOTICES

The Obituary Notice or death notice in the local paper is a matter for careful consideration. The simple announcement which gives the essential information is the best. In some cases, a funeral director is requested to insert over-sentimental verses, and all the funeral director's tact is called upon to dissuade the family in their own interest.

The family may ask for insertions in certain national papers or in a district town where they have connections. The funeral director should offer to do this for them.

. The family should be advised that no times can be inserted until they have agreed with the minister concerned.

Certain national papers have strict regulations as to the sequence to be followed in a death notice. The order is usually as follows: surname, date of death, place of death, Christian names of deceased, age, relationship to next-of-kin, private address, funeral arrangements (see Obituary Notice).

If the deceased was well known, it is a service to the family to advise press reporters of the death and to submit such information as the family may wish to furnish for the purpose of a news paragraph.

OBITUARY NOTICE

There is an urgency about this matter, for the family usually expect the notice to be in the first available issue of the newspaper selected for use. Also, publishers have a time limit for accepting notices.

Yet there are several items which require attention before the notice may be inserted. These items are:

CLERGY: Day, time, and details of the service must be confirmed with the minister concerned.

CREMATORIUM: Day and time of cremation must be fixed with the Crematorium Superintendent.

CEMETERY: The day and time should also be confirmed with the cemetery office.

As stated in the section on Press Notices the obituary notice, or death notice, in the local paper is a matter for careful consideration. Many local newspapers have no established order, but national papers, such as *The Times* and the *Daily Telegraph*, have unwritten rules which have been evolved through many years to facilitate trouble-free publication of notices. Since these notices are essentially factual they are edited as necessary to a set style. The main rules observed by the *Daily Telegraph*, which are familiar to many funeral directors, to whom they are known as the "Telegraph Order", are given below.

The Editor of the *Daily Telegraph* points out that they are not absolute since a situation can arise where either there is a special reason for waiving a particular rule or there is no rule to cover the exact circumstances when an *ad hoc* ruling must be made.

Death notices received by post must be signed by a relative or executor unless received from a funeral director, advertising agent, solicitor, or from another newspaper.

Telephoned notices are accepted only from subscribers whose names and addresses can be checked in the telephone directory and who can be telephoned back for confirmation. If the originator of the notice is not a funeral director or a relative, confirmation has to be made with a member of the family.

All notices commence with the proper surname of the deceased (professional names are included in brackets if required) and continue with the date of death, which must appear, unless it is not possible to ascertain it.

The exact time of death is not included, nor are thanks to the doctor and staff of hospitals and nursing homes.

The request for other papers to copy is not permitted.

The name of a nursing home or hotel cannot appear without its approval. The name of a hospital is not mentioned in conjunction with either of the phrases "after an operation" or "as the result of an accident" unless, in the case of an accident, it is made clear that it did not take place in the hospital.

Illnesses and diseases are not mentioned by name.

Lengthy descriptions of the deceased's career and achievements, more suited to an editorial obituary notice, are not normally included in paid-for death notices.

There is no objection to a farewell message at the end of the notice (for example, a Biblical quotation or Latin tag) but for reasons of space it should be as short as possible.

Only one notice of the same death is published in any one issue. If more than one is received, precedence is given to the one from the nearest relative. The others may, if required, appear in subsequent issues.

SUMMARY

THE ANNOUNCEMENT OF DEATH

1. Family Name (Surname)	As the heading of the notice
2. When	On April 8—the day of the week is normally omitted
3. How (if desired) for example	Passed peacefully away, After a long/short illness (bravely borne), Suddenly, As the result of a street accident, etc.
4. Where: for example	At . . . (his home), In hospital/a nursing home, At Dover,
5. Who: for example	(Captain) John Smith, M.B.E., M.A. (The family name is normally repeated in the body of the notice, either here or after husband/wife of . . .)
6. Age (if desired)	or possibly later—see 12
7. Husband/Wife of (if desired)	Husband, dear/beloved/much loved husband of . . . Smith
8. Address	of . . . (if not already given as place of death)
9. Former Address (if desired)	e.g. Formerly of Calcutta

10. Other Relationship	Family name of married daughters are often added
11. Business Connections or Special Distinctions (if desired)	Director/Manager of . . . Past Master of . . .
12. Age	(if not put in earlier, may go here)

THE FUNERAL

If funeral arrangements are to be announced continue as follows:

13. Place of Service	Funeral Service at St John's Church, Cremation at . . . etc.
14. Day and Time of Service	e.g. on Friday May 18 at 2.30 p.m., followed by . . . at . . .
15. Place of Burial or Cremation	(if service has been in church)
16. Requests *re* letters or mourning (if any)	
17. Arrangements *re* receipt of flowers (if any)	
18. Text (if desired)	(This may appear after 12, if the funeral is not to be announced)

Funeral Rites (Anglican)

The Anglican Church, whose members are commonly described as "C. of E." is, in fact, represented in Great Britain by the Church of England, the Church in Wales, the Episcopal Church in Scotland, and the Church in Ireland (which covers both Northern Ireland and the Republic of Ireland).

The forms of Service of the Church of England are regulated by English law as it is officially the Established Church. All parish churchyards are under its control, but their use is also available to other Christians.

The authorized form of Anglican services is to be found in the Book of Common Prayer of 1662. A revision of this was approved by the Church, but rejected by Parliament, in 1928. In spite of this rejection the 1928 Prayer Book is used in the majority of churches. The funeral Service therein described and normally used is as follows: the officiating clergyman meets the coffin at the churchyard gate or at the church door and reads the "opening sentence", while the mourners follow in procession. The coffin is placed with the foot towards the altar normally below the chancel steps, but in some churches it can only be accommodated in the chancel. (In the case of a priest the head of the coffin is placed towards the altar. When the body of a vicar is taken into his own church, his own stall is always left vacant.) When the coffin is in position and the mourners have taken their places, the church service is begun by the reading of a psalm (the Prayer Book gives three alternatives and others are also used). This is followed by a Lesson, normally one of the four alternatives in the Prayer Book, but again, others may be used. This is followed by the Lord's Prayer, a set of Versicles and Responses, and the service is concluded by the Blessing.

The sentences and prayers which comprise the committal service are taken at the grave-side in cases of burial. The coffin is normally lowered into the grave immediately upon arrival at the grave or at the end of the preliminary quotations, either at the words "... to fall from thee", or "... and his righteousness upon children's children". Earth is required to cast thrice on to the coffin with the words: "Earth to earth, ashes to ashes, dust to dust." This is normally done by a cemetery or churchyard official, but it is necessary for the funeral director to check on this in advance and to have earth ready to do it himself if required. In some districts the mourners then follow this lead and also cast earth on the coffin.

For cremation the same Order of Service is used, the clergyman simply modifying the actual words of committal and reading, "We therefore commit this body to the elements" (or "to the flames" or "to be burned") then omitting the words "earth to earth", thus leaving the quite suitable "ashes to ashes, dust to dust". At the moment of committal the coffin moves towards the committal chamber or is hidden from view by the closing of curtains.

When the whole funeral service is held in the crematorium chapel, the committal is combined in the service rather than taken as a separate part as is the case at the grave-side. The actual point at which the committal is performed varies at the discretion of the clergyman; it may be at the end of the service or before the prayers.

Quite commonly one or two hymns are added to the above service and an address is also frequently included. In a full choral service the psalm would also be sung and the Nunc Dimittis would be sung at the end as the procession leaves. Sometimes an anthem is sung by the choir alone in place of a hymn. Opening and closing organ Voluntaries may also be used at a church service when nothing is to be sung.

8

The existence of set prayers, etc., makes it possible to print full service sheets if desired.

For church members the funeral service is very frequently taken in their parish church, but since the majority of non-church-going English claim a Church of England funeral, the simple read service at a cemetery chapel is more common. The Church of England sections of cemeteries are consecrated by a bishop and are referred to as Consecrated Ground. (See *Alternative Services: Second Series*, pp. 101–138.)

Death Grant, etc.

LIABILITY BY DATE OF BIRTH

The Death Grant is a sum of money payable on the death of an insured man, his wife, child, or widow, or of an insured woman, her husband, child, or widower, subject to certain conditions under the National Assistance Act, 1948. It is important to note that the Death Grant *cannot* be paid for the death of:

> a man born before 5 July 1883
> a woman born before 5 July 1888
> a stillborn child

AMOUNTS PAYABLE

The amount of the Death Grant payable depends on the age of the person and the number of contributions paid. The full amounts of the Death Grant payable when contributions are fully satisfied are as follows:

1. In respect of a person over 18 (excluding a man born before 5 July 1893 or a woman born before 5 July 1898) the amount is £25.
2. In respect of a man born between 5 July 1883 and 1893 or a woman born between 5 July 1888 and 1898 the

amount is £12 10s. This is because the Death Grant was not provided under State Insurance schemes and only National Insurance contributions since 5 July 1948 count toward it.

3. In respect of a person under 18 the amount is:

For a child under 3 years   £7 10s.
For a child 3 to 5 years (inclusive)   £12 10s.
For a child 6 to 17 years (inclusive) £8 15s.

It is to be noted that the amount paid to the claimant may also be limited to the amount of the funeral expenses where they are less than the full rate of the grant payable.

The Death Grant is not part of a deceased person's estate and therefore is not liable for estate duty.

CONTRIBUTION CONDITIONS

There are two contribution conditions which must be satisfied. First, at least twenty-six contributions of any class must have been paid or credited since 5 July 1948 (in the original Act these contributions had to be paid); and secondly at least forty-five contributions of any class must have been paid or credited in the last complete contribution year before the date on which the conditions have to be satisfied.

If the first condition is not satisfied, no grant can be paid. If the first condition is satisfied, but the second is not, there is an alternative condition which can be applied, namely that an average of at least forty-five contributions a year has been paid or credited between 5 July 1948 (or sixteenth birthday, if later) and the end of the last complete contribution year before the date on which the conditions have to be satisfied. In this case a full Death Grant can be paid, but if the average is less than forty-five, but not less than thirteen, a reduced grant may be paid.

It is to be noted that contributions may be credited as distinct from paid, for weeks of sickness or unemployment, for weeks in which the widow's benefit is being paid, and for weeks of full time education under the age of eighteen.

In the case of a man the contribution conditions may be satisfied either on his own insurance record or on that of his wife, whether she is still living or not. In a case of a woman the conditions may be satisfied on her own insurance record or on that of her husband, whether he is still living or not. If her marriage has been terminated by divorce or has been annulled, and she has not remarried, her former husband's record may be used to help to satisfy the contribution conditions. In connection with a child the contribution conditions are normally satisfied on the insurance record of the father or mother with whom the child was living, or of another person of whose family the child was a member, in accordance with the provisions of the Family Allowance Acts.

Where contribution conditions cannot be satisfied in the case of a child on any other person's insurance record, then a grant, or the amount of funeral expenses if less, may in certain circumstances be paid.

CLAIMS PROCEDURE

The Registrar of Deaths will provide a special death certificate free of charge for national insurance purposes (see Registration of Deaths). A claim should be made within six months after the date of death but it is advisable to lodge the claim as soon as possible. The person making a claim should provide the following documents (if they are to hand or can be obtained easily): Death Certificate; the deceased's National Insurance contribution card, Birth Certificate, and Marriage Certificate; any National Insurance or Family Allowance order book or Welfare Foods Service books relating to the deceased. If a claim is being made for funeral expenses, the funeral director's account or estimate will be needed; in order to assist members in this direction the National Association of Funeral Directors supplies a special form for use by an executor or other person (other than the next-of-kin) to show that the cost of the funeral was over £25, or an exact figure, if less.

From time to time representations have been made to the Ministry of Pensions and National Insurance for the Death Grant to be made payable to the funeral director, but this has always been refused on the ground that the Death Grant is a payment to the deceased's personal representative to meet expenses in connection with the funeral which need not necessarily be the cost of the funeral itself. The Ministry points out that, quite apart from other considerations, Section 32 of the National Insurance Act, 1946, specifically lays down that every agreement to assign a National Insurance Benefit shall be void.

Any National Insurance contribution card belonging to the deceased should be sent to the local office of the Ministry of Pensions and National Insurance together with the date of death.

Further information may be obtained from Leaflet N.I.49 or from the local office of the Ministry of Pensions and National Insurance and if the address is unknown this may be obtained from the local Post Office.

Bank Accounts and Pensions

When notice of the death of a customer is received by the bank, no further withdrawals can be allowed on the account, whether it be in credit or overdrawn, if the account is in the sole name of the deceased, but on occasions a widow could probably arrange with her late husband's bank manager to open an account in her name on the basis of a temporary overdraft until the estate has been proved. Obviously this facility would depend on the amount of the overdraft required, the size of the estate, and the terms of the will (if any). In the case of a joint account showing a credit balance at the time of the death of one of the parties, the survivor can continue to operate the account provided this was covered in the mandate given by the original account holders, but this would not, of course, imply that the survivor is necessarily entitled to the balance. Generally speaking, if the account stands at more than £300, then half the amount of the account at the time of death may be taken into account in arriving at death duties. The same rules apply to Trustee Savings Banks and to Post Office Savings Banks.

PENSIONS

With regard to the Old Age Pension, this ceases at the time of death and any amount due would be paid by the Post Office if the Pension Book had been signed, otherwise the claimant should send the Pension Book, together with a copy of the Death Certificate, to the local office of the Ministry of Pensions and National Insurance, which will then pay the outstanding arrears. So far as other pensions payments are concerned, these depend entirely on the conditions of the pension scheme concerned.

WIDOW'S BENEFITS

Every widow under the age of sixty, whose husband satisfied the necessary contributions under the National Insurance scheme is entitled to receive a weekly benefit, called the *widow's allowance* for the first thirteen weeks after her husband's death. After that the payment of further widow's benefit depends on individual circumstances such as family responsibilities and age (see Leaflet N.I.13). She may also be entitled to an Industrial Injuries Death Benefit if her husband's death was due to an accident at work or a prescribed industrial disease (see Leaflet N.I.10). This benefit is paid only to the lawful widow. A woman whose marriage has been dissolved by divorce or annulment is, in law, not the widow of her former husband. If the widow is an old age pensioner she may be eligible for an increase in her retirement pension (see Leaflet N.I.15).

For further information or help on any matter arising in connection with the National Insurance scheme contact should be made with the local office of the Ministry of Pensions and National Insurance, the address of which (if unknown) can be obtained from the local Post Office.

Registration of Deaths

The death of every person dying in England and Wales and the cause thereof shall be registered by the Registrar of Births and Death for the sub-district in which death occurred.

It is the duty of the person qualified and liable to register (the Informant) to give the Registrar, before the expiration of five days from the date of death, information to the best of his knowledge and belief of the particulars required to be registered concerning the death, and in the presence of the Registrar to sign the register.

LIABILITY TO REGISTER

If for some reason the death cannot be registered within five days, fourteen days are allowed providing a qualified informant has sent a written notification of the death to the Registrar together with the appropriate written notice of the signing of the Medical Certificate of the Cause of Death.

REGISTRAR'S CERTIFICATE FOR BURIAL OR CREMATION

(NOTE: This certificate was formerly named the Disposal Certificate and is still frequently referred to as such.)

Upon registering a death the Registrar must give to the person giving the information concerning the death (the Informant) a certificate under his hand that he has registered the death. Such certificate is called *Certificate for Burial or Cremation* (issued after registration).

In certain circumstances the Registrar can issue a *Certificate for Burial* (issued *before* registration) as stated on the certificate; this is not acceptable for cremation. It is usually issued when the Informant is temporarily unable to attend at the Registrar's Office, a duty he must still fulfil within fourteen days. Before issuing such a certificate the Registrar requires to have received a properly completed Medical Certificate of the Cause of Death. In these circumstances the certificate may be collected from the Registrar by the funeral director, if desired.

It is a useful means of avoiding delay, for it authorizes removal from any hospital and allows the commencement of preservative treatment.

In this certificate provision is made for the completion of either form of certificate on the one document which the Informant is instructed to hand on to the funeral director. He in turn must hand it to the Cemetery Registrar, or at the churchyard to the Vicar, or to the Medical Referee in the case of cremation.

DEATH CERTIFICATES AND COPIES FOR LEGAL PURPOSES

The Registrar will also issue, at the time of registration or later, at a small charge, certified copies of the entry in the register (Death Certificates for legal purposes), modified certificates for claims on Friendly Societies, and a special free Death Certificate for claiming the National Insurance Death Grant when applicable. Additional Death Certificates required more than six months after death are obtainable from the Registrar-General, Somerset House, London, W.C.2, at a nominal charge.

Coroner's Procedure

DUTY TO REPORT CERTAIN DEATHS TO CORONER

The law makes it the duty of the Registrar to report certain cases to the Coroner and defines the circumstances which govern this duty as follows:

1. Where the deceased was not attended during his last illness by a registered medical practitioner;

2. If the Registrar has been unable to obtain delivery of a duly completed Medical Certificate of the Cause of Death;

3. Where it appears to the Registrar from the particulars contained in the Medical Certificate, or otherwise, that the deceased was not seen by any certifying practitioner *either after* death *or* within *fourteen days before* death;

4. Where the cause of death appears to be unknown;

5. If the Registrar has reason to believe that the death was unnatural or directly, or indirectly, caused by any sort of accident, violence, or neglect, or was attended by suspicious circumstances; it is the practice for any death occurring within a year of a fracture to be reported;

6. Where the death occurred after an operation necessitated by injury, or under an operation, or before recovery from the effects of the anaesthetic; or

7. If it appears to the Registrar from the contents of any Medical Certificate that the death was due to abortion, industrial disease, or poisoning (including industrial or food poisoning), or circumstances of military service which may have accelerated or caused death.

In addition the law also provides that certain persons have a statutory duty to inform the Coroner of a death. These are:

1. The Governor of a prison: whenever a death occurs in any sort of H.M. Prisons, the Coroner must hold a full inquest.

2. The person in charge of a mental hospital must report the death of any certified mental patient to the Coroner, who must also be informed of the death of any temporary patient who dies in an unregistered hospital or in a nursing home.

In the latter case the duty lies with the doctor who attended the patient during his last illness.

Stillbirth

DEFINITION

"Stillborn child" means a child born dead after the twenty-eighth week of pregnancy.

Children born dead before the twenty-eighth week of pregnancy are outside the Act and there is no legislation relating to the disposal of the body.

CERTIFICATION

The Registrar must receive

either

1. A satisfactory Certificate of Stillbirth issued by a doctor or certified midwife.

or

2. The informant shall make a statutory declaration "to the effect that no registered medical practitioner or certified midwife was present at the birth or has examined the

body, or that his or her certificate cannot be obtained, and that the child was not born alive".

REGISTRATION

The persons qualified to inform the Registrar are:

1. The father (of a legitimate child only).
2. The mother.
3. The occupier of the house in which the birth occurred, or in the case of an institution, the Chief Resident Officer.
4. If all the former default, any person present at the birth.

On the receipt of satisfactory information in the prescribed form the Registrar issues a Certificate for Burial or Cremation.

STILLBIRTHS AND THE CORONER

A stillbirth cannot be the subject of a complete inquest because there has been no independent life and therefore no subsequent death. Yet cases come to the notice of the Coroner because some suspicion attaches to the birth of the infant.

Should it be established that the child was in fact stillborn, the Coroner issues his Burial Order or Certificate E and informs the Registrar of the stillbirth.

Law and Practice of Burial

RIGHT OF CHRISTIAN BURIAL

All the following relates to the Burial Service of the Church of England, the clergy of which are subject to legal obligations.

Everyone dying in this country, and not within certain exclusions laid down by ecclesiastical law, has a right to a Christian burial. But the question arises, What is a "Christian Burial"? By some authorities the words are taken as equivalent to burial with a full Form of Burial Service appearing in the Book of Common Prayer. The rubric at the head of "The Order for the Burial of the Dead" which was added in 1662 and has the statutory authority of the Act of Uniformity recites that, "here it is to be noted that the Office ensuing is not to be used for any that die unbaptized, or excommunicate, or have laid violent hands upon themselves".

It has been decided in the clearest possible fashion that a clergyman cannot legally refuse to read the Burial Service, when required to do so, over (a) a Dissenter or a Dissenter's child and (b) a person who has only received baptism and has not been subsequently received into the Church. A child baptized by a Nonconformist minister is NOT an unbaptized person within the meaning of the rubric of 1662.

The word "excommunicate" in the rubric is to be construed as referring to the major excommunication mentioned in Canon 68 of 1603. Excommunication as far as the Church of England is concerned is to-day obsolete.

The provision concerning those laying hands upon themselves is unhappily of frequent concern. Persons who lay violent hands upon themselves are of more than one class. Some fall within the definition of suicide which in criminal law was a felony, that of self-murder, until the enactment of the Suicide Act of 1961. Stephen in *Digest of Criminal Law* says: "A person who kills himself in a manner which in the case of another person would amount to murder is guilty of murder. A person cannot commit manslaughter on himself." And Harris in *Criminal Law* says: "Suicide is the felony of murder inasmuch as it is the murder of one of the sovereign's subjects. To be such an offence, the act must be committed deliberately and by one who has arrived at years of discretion, and is in his right mind."

Conviction of the crime of self-murder is by determination of a Coroner's Inquest. A person found by a Coroner's Inquest to have committed *felo de se* was before the nineteenth century in England buried according to rude practice, without religious ceremony in a public highway at the cross-roads with a stake driven through the body, and his goods and chattels were forfeited to the Crown. This custom was abolished by the Interments (Felo de se) Act of 1882.

The above dire consequences were averted by a verdict of suicide "whilst in the condition of temporary insanity" or as it is phrased by many of our juries to-day "whilst the balance of his mind was disturbed".

Dealing with these cases is distressing for all concerned, and it is always advisable to give to the minister, who is to take the funeral service, the fullest possible details, so that he can decide upon his course of action. Special difficulties can be met by the authorization by the Diocesan (the Bishop) of a special Form of Service for particular cases. (See *Alternative Services: Second Series*, pp. 114–15.)

BURIAL LAWS AMENDMENT ACT, 1880

This Act made very important alterations in the law as to burial services in accordance with the ritual of the Church of England. Before it was passed, the reading of that service was compulsory for burial in consecrated ground. It was also illegal for an unauthorized person to read the Burial Service at a burial in consecrated ground and for a clergyman to read the Burial Service over the burial in unconsecrated ground. This Act allows of burial in consecrated ground without the Church of England Service and in unconsecrated ground with it. Thus there is now complete freedom to bury in consecrated ground with or without the Service if the provisions of the Act are followed.

Any relative, friend, or legal representative having the charge of, or being responsible for, the burial of a deceased person may give forty-eight hours' notice in writing, endorsed on the outside "Notice of Burial" to, or leave or cause the same to be left at the usual place of residence of, the rector, vicar, or other incumbent, or in his absence the officiating minister in charge of any parish or ecclesiastical district or place, or any person appointed by him to receive such notice, that it is intended that such deceased shall be buried within the churchyard or grave-yard of such parish or ecclesiastical district or place without the performance, in the manner prescribed by law, of the Service for the Burial of the dead according to the rites of the Church of England, and after receiving such Notice no rector, vicar, incumbent, or officiating minister shall be liable to any censure or penalty, ecclesiastical or civil, for permitting any such burial as aforesaid. Such notice shall be in writing, plainly signed with the name and stating the address of the person giving it, *and shall be in the form or to the effect of Schedule (A) annexed to this Act.*

To-day this applies only to burials in churchyards under the care of an incumbent who insists on the Notice in due form. Generally speaking incumbents no longer insist on a Notice in writing and permission is more often than not given over the telephone.

All regulations as to the position and marking of the grave which would be in force in such churchyards, or grave-yards in the case of persons interred therein with the Service of the Church of England, shall be in force as to burials under the Act; any person who, if the burial had taken place with the Service of the Church of England, would have been entitled by law to receive any fee shall be entitled under this Act to receive the like fee in respect thereof.

BURIALS IN CHURCHYARDS

There exists in theory a right for all parishioners to be buried free in their parish churchyards. Practically speaking, however, appropriate fees to clergyman and sexton in accordance with the Official List (now, presumably, the 1962 Order) are extracted and are compulsory. Subject to such fees, however, the right exists and is safeguarded by Canon 68. It is enjoyed by all Christians, including Nonconformist Christians and by persons baptized by Noncon-

formists. Jews and other non-Christians do not enjoy this
right and generally speaking they are usually buried in
burial grounds appropriate to their faith.

The right is one of burial only and does not extend to the
right of burial in a particular place therein. The site of the
grave is fixed by the incumbent.

The person paying fees for a burial does not obtain owner-
ship of the grave, nor even, in strict law, the exclusive right
of burial therein. All land in a churchyard remains the
property of the Church authorities unless granted to an individual by faculty. There are therefore no grave-deeds.

By custom, permission is implied to erect a memorial of
such shape and material, and with inscription, as the incumbent may approve as the representative of the Chancel-
lor of the Diocese, to whom there is a right of appeal. This
seems to imply recognition of a customary right of exclusive
burial. The ancient common law right of burial of a
parishioner can, however, be held to apply as long as there
is room for any such burial in any grave unreserved by
faculty, whether marked by a memorial or not. No modern
application of this right is known.

A person who has previously paid either burial or monumental fees in respect of a grave has, however, no apparent
right to be consulted before it is used for a further burial.

PAROCHIAL FEES

There is still no uniformity in the amount charged in
different parishes in the matter of fees for burial. A further
attempt was made in 1962 to achieve uniformity, but the
recommendations have not, as yet, been universally accepted
by all clergy. The new measures are of first importance to
funeral directors and details are fully given below:

PAROCHIAL FEES ORDER, 1962

The Order, a Statutory Instrument, which is made under
Ecclesiastical Fees Measure, 1962 (10 and 11, Eliz. 2 No. 1)
was drafted by the Church Commissioners for England, and

approved by the Church Assembly and by Parliament. It applies to all parishes and churches of the Church of England in the Provinces of Canterbury and York, except the Isle of Man and the Channel Islands, but in parishes which did not adopt the Commissioners' formal scale of fees, use of the new schedule is not compulsory until there is a change of vicar or rector. It lays down a scale of fees payable to the vicar, Church officials, and Parochial Church Councils in respect of, among other things, funeral services, burials, the burial of cremated remains, and monuments. A scale of Church fees for funeral services is an innovation, as is also the inclusion of a fixed maintenance payment to the Parochial Church Council; also the single class of monumental fees.

It should be noted that the lack of either clerk or sexton does not reduce the fee, the amount involved going to the vicar. Responsibility for arranging the digging of the grave is placed upon the person having charge of the funeral.

The most surprising point arises from the Explanatory Notes issued with the Order by the Church Commissioners. Therein "persons having a right by law or by custom to be buried in the churchyard" are defined. They are defined as follows:

1. Parishioners (which term includes persons dying in the parish);
2. Non-parishioners who nevertheless have a statutory right, (e.g. under the New Parishes Measure 1943, on the formation of a new parish); and
3. Persons customarily regarded as parishioners (for example, parishioners and non-parishioners for whom family graves or vaults are to be opened or whose close relatives have been buried in the churchyard).

PARISHIONERS

The terms parishioner and resident are normally regarded as synonymous, but the definite inclusion as parishioners of persons dying within the parish is against common practice, although not wholly unknown, but does agree with the books on Law of Burial, which quote it as a definite ancient right, now lapsed into the realms of theory, like that of free burial of parishioners. Fellows states that it has never been authoritatively tested in the courts. Its resurrection is therefore surprising.

NON-PARISHIONERS

This is in accord with strict Burial Law and precedent, but in practice the burial rights of ex-parishioners, transferred to a new churchyard-less parish, are often denied them.

PERSONS CUSTOMARILY REGARDED AS PARISHIONERS

This is a most important and revolutionary definition. It appears to break new ground indeed for it means that all these people are unconditionally entitled to be buried in the churchyard at the parishioner rate of fees, and that especially the non-parishioner reopening fee will rarely apply. It conflicts very sharply with normal churchyard practice, and goes beyond any definition given in books on Law of Burial. The right of burial of a non-parishioner in the grave of a near member of the family is generally accepted, but no right to the parishioner rate of fees in such instance has been stated before. Moreover, the wording here seems to state a right for such a person to be buried at parishioner rates if necessary in a new grave, which is entirely without precedent, and probably contrary to the Commissioner's intention.

Funeral directors will undoubtedly feel it their duty to ensure that their clients obtain full benefit of their every right, and they will doubtless take up these points with local parishes.

The burial of persons not in the above categories requires the consent of the incumbent and of the Parochial Church Council, who are free to fix the fees to be charged.

Some town vicars, who have no churchyards, are far from

9

happy about the high cost of a full Church service, fearing that funerals will less often be brought into church. Some already claim their full entitlement. Others are deciding what is suitable to each case, while others again are making no change. The same sort of thing is happening where there are churchyards. Here, some even go for the best of both worlds, adding any increased items to old substantial fees. The result is most confusing to the conscientious funeral director who wishes to give his clients a precise idea of their financial commitments, and incidentally to cover himself against any disputes. Funeral directors are well advised to check parish policy on this.

NOTE: The standardized monumental fees are included in the Summary of main charges for information (see page 117).

BURIALS IN CEMETERIES

The various Burial Acts have from time to time removed the authority for the provision of burial grounds from the Ecclesiastical Authority to the Civil Authority. It is seldom that difficulties in law arise in the case of interments in either privately owned or civic cemeteries. Many of the private cemeteries are governed by their own special Act of Parliament and the civic cemeteries by the Burial Acts and the Public Health Acts, and they make regulations in accordance with these Acts for the good conduct and smooth running of the cemeteries in the best interests of the public. The owners of cemeteries, whether a private company or a local authority, fix their own fees. Usually they publish brochures listing their charges and regulations. In most municipal authority cemeteries a higher scale of fees applies for the burial of non-parishioners (unless ratepayers). Some make concessions for former parishioners or for the relatives of parishioners.

All public and most private cemeteries have sections of both consecrated (C. of E.) and general ground. Some also have Roman Catholic sections, and occasionally there are

	TO WHOM PAYABLE				
	Vicar	Clerk	Sexton	P.C.C.	Total
1. Church Fees for a Funeral Service					
(a) Without organ	£1	10s.	10s.	10s.	£2 10s.
(b) With organ (organist's and choir fees extra)	£2	£1	10s.	£1	£4 10s.
2. Church and Burial Fees—for earth grave or vault, or burial of cremated remains					
(1) With a service in the church (also applying in cases of cremation with burial of cremated remains later)					
(a) Without organ	£1	10s.	10s.	£1 10s.	£3 10s.
(b) With organ (organist's and choir fees extra)	£2	£1	10s.	£2	£5 10s.
(2) Without use of church	£1	10s.	10s.	£1	£3 10s.
(3) Stillborn child	£1				
Digging charges (the vicar and P.C.C. may fix the charge if a Church official is the digger). Additional to the above					
This scale of burial fees relates to persons having a right by law to be buried in the churchyard.					
3. Monumental Fees					
(a) Any new monument, including inscription	£3		10s.	£2	£5 10s.
(b) Additional inscription	£1 5s.		2s.		£1 7s.
(c) Small wooden cross					

sections reserved for other religious groups. A few private cemeteries are run by religious organizations for the sole use of their own members.

Cemeteries normally offer two types of grave in each section of ground.

1. Public, or common, graves in which the bodies of a number of unrelated persons are buried together, without any further rights in respect of the grave being granted to the person paying the fees.

2. Private, or Faculty, graves, whereof the person paying the fees is granted the freehold and sole burial rights. Private grave plots are valued according to their accessibility. In most cemeteries choice of position, as well as of price, is possible. The maximum number of burials permitted varies and may be limited by the nature of the site. The legal minimum depth of burial requires three feet of earth between the coffin and the normal ground level. In practice a deficiency of a few inches is often permitted, provided that the coffin is covered with concrete.

Under Ecclesiastical Law a Faculty of the Ordinary, issued by the Diocesan Registrar, is always required before a body can be removed from one consecrated place of burial to another; but in practice cemeteries frequently act on a Home Office Licence.

Except in such cases as above no exhumation shall take place without a Licence issued by one of Her Majesty's Principal Secretaries of State. The present cost is £2 and the Licence is obtainable from the Home Office.

BURIALS IN CONSECRATED BUILDINGS

As far as the law is concerned, there have been a number of interesting cases to settle disputes about burial in churches and the like, but in fact to-day such right as an incumbent might have had to consent to burial within a church without a Faculty has become obsolete, and Faculties to permit such cases are rarely, if ever, granted. By the Public Health

Act of 1875 burials within or underneath churches in urban areas were prohibited. Burial in St Paul's Cathedral or Westminster Abbey is only by invitation under Her Majesty's Royal Sign Manual.

BURIALS IN PRIVATE GROUNDS

Burial in private ground, other than a church or a cemetery, is not forbidden by law. No NEW private grounds can be opened without the consent of the Minister of Housing and Local Government. Burials in private grounds must be registered under the Registrations of Burials Acts, 1864.

MONUMENTAL RESTRICTIONS

An increasing number of dioceses restrict churchyard memorials to headstones of specified materials. The lawn cemeteries or lawn sections in cemeteries, which have the same type of restrictions, are becoming common. Clients are entitled to be informed of any such restriction of their choice of memorial before coming to a decision on the place of burial.

Law and Practice of Cremation

STATUTORY FORMS

No cremation shall take place unless the required forms have been completed except by order of the Secretary of State. It is to be noted that the Statutory Forms vary slightly as each crematorium authority issues its own Form, and the Home Office has ruled that although the statutory requirements may be added to at the discretion of the crematorium authority none may be omitted. There are normally four forms to be completed as follows:

Form A—Application for Cremation. This is completed by the next-of-kin or the executor (unless there is good reason why this cannot be done). It must also be countersigned by one of the persons whose qualifications are listed on the form.[1]

Form B—Certificate of Medical Attendant. This is completed by the medical practitioner who attended the deceased during his last illness and who issues the Certificate of the Cause of Death.

Form C—Confirmatory Medical Certificates. This is completed by a registered medical practitioner of not less than five years' standing. He must not be a relative of the deceased nor a relative or partner of the doctor completing Form B.

Form F—Authority to Cremate. This is completed by the Medical Referee.

DISPOSAL OF CREMATED REMAINS[2]

After the cremation of a deceased person, the remains must be given into the charge of the person who applied for the cremation, if he so desires. If not, they must be retained by the cremation authority, and, in the absence of any special arrangements, must be decently interred in a burial ground, or scattered. If left in temporary deposit and not removed within a reasonable time, a fortnight's notice must be given to the person who applied for the cremation, before the remains are interred or scattered.

All crematoria provide forms to enable the applicant to express his wishes as to the disposal of cremated remains.

Cremated remains are legally not a body. The Registration Act, 1926, infers that disposal of the body is achieved by cremation. No law regulates the disposal of cremated remains, but it is affected by certain regulations of the Anglican Church mentioned below. It should, however, be noted that cremated remains are, in law, treated as a body for exhumation.

NORMAL METHODS OF DISPOSAL

The four normal methods of the disposal of cremated remains are as follows:

1. *Scattering* (the Anglican Church officially uses the term "Strewing"). This is by far the most common method. Gardens of Remembrance are available for this purpose at all crematoria, wherein usually the family may choose, but not mark, the place. Scattering may also take place on family graves in cemeteries, on common land, in gardens, over water, from aircraft, etc.; but in most English dioceses scattering in a churchyard is forbidden. It is usually acceptable, however, to overcome this ban by lifting a turf and scattering beneath it. Scattering is absolutely forbidden by the Church in Wales.

2. *Burial.* Caskets of cremated remains may be buried in the grounds of most crematoria. Many churchyards and some cemeteries have special sections for such burials, or offer a small plot for that purpose. Burial is also possible in any existing family grave, even when no space remains for further earth burial (this is frequently a reason for cremation), but in a closed churchyard a Faculty is required. Burial in consecrated ground is the official recommendation of the Anglican Church. Crematorium grounds are, of course, dedicated, not consecrated, since they must be available to all. Burial inside a consecrated building is rare, and requires a Faculty.

3. *Deposit in a Niche.* Many Crematoria, and all of the older ones, have a columbarium in which there are niches for the permanent deposit of urns and cremated remains. Such deposit is also possible in some churches.

4. *By storage.* Retention in a temporary deposit of cremated remains either by a crematorium or by a funeral director until the final disposal is decided, or until a further death makes mingling possible, is common.

MEMORIAL INSCRIPTIONS AT CREMATORIA

Clients are entitled to be informed of the available methods of memorial inscriptions at the crematorium of their choice, which are likely to include the following:

Inscription in the Book of Memory (or Book of Remembrance);
Individual inscription (wall tablet, flagstone, etc.);
Inscription on the roll of Recordia.

FEES

Charges vary slightly at each crematorium. Many items are subject to Ministry approval. Each crematorium publishes its regulations and fees, and copies can be obtained on application.

PART THREE

Spiritual Letters of
Consolation

"O my God, let me never forget that seasons of consolation are refreshments here, and nothing more; not our abiding state. They will not remain with us, except in heaven. Here they are only intended to prepare us for doing and suffering. I pray Thee, O God, to give them to me from time to time. Shed over me the sweetness of Thy Presence, lest I faint by the way; lest I find religious service wearisome, through my exceeding infirmity, and give over prayer and meditation; lest I go about my daily work in a dry spirit, or am tempted to take pleasure in it for its own sake, and not for Thee. Give me Thy Divine consolations from time to time. . . . let them carry me forward to the thought and desire of heaven."

JOHN HENRY NEWMAN

"Listen! I will unfold a mystery: we shall not all die, but we shall all be changed in a flash, in the twinkling of an eye, at the last trumpet call. For the trumpet will sound, and the dead will rise immortal, and we shall be changed. This perishable being must be clothed with the imperishable, and what is mortal must be clothed with immortality. And when our mortality has been clothed with immortality, then the saying of Scripture will come true: 'Death is swallowed up; victory is won!' 'O Death, where is your victory? O Death, where is your sting?' The sting of death is sin, and sin gains its power from the law; but, God be praised, he gives us the victory through our Lord Jesus Christ.

Therefore my beloved brothers, stand firm and immovable, and work for the Lord always, work without limit, since you know that in the Lord your labour cannot be lost." *1 Cor. 15.51–8 (N.E.B.)*

Can I see another's woe,
And not be in sorrow too?
Can I see another's grief,
And not seek for kind relief?

Can I see a falling tear,
And not feel my sorrow's share? ...

He doth give his joy to all:
He becomes an infant small,
He becomes a man of woe,
He doth feel the sorrow too.

WILLIAM BLAKE

Peace is my parting gift to you, my own peace, such as the world cannot give. Set your troubled hearts at rest, and banish your fears.   *John 14.27 (N.E.B.)*

Spiritual Letters of Consolation

ARCHBISHOP FÉNELON

To a nobleman, on the death of his son

I think continually of your sorrow.... Prayer is the only comfort; in that alone we are wholly with God. So soon as we are with Him by union of the heart and simple faith, we pray; and all other things, however holy, if they check that intercourse, become rather study than prayer. And none save the Comforter can soothe sorrow. Let us, then, abide silently before Him; He will comfort us, and we shall find all, and more than we have lost, in Him. This is a true and inexhaustible Consolation.

To Nicolas de Harlai Bonneuil, on the death of his son-in-law, the Marquis de Crèvecoeur   12 November 1701

I am deeply touched at your loss ... I would I could be at hand to share your grief and endeavour to comfort you. But you know whence comes all true consolation in the loss of those who are dear to us. Religion can give no better comfort than in telling us that we have not lost them, and that there is a home to which we are daily drawing nearer, in which we shall all meet again. So let us not sorrow as those who have no hope. I am deprived of the pleasure of seeing you, but I call to mind how fast life flows away, and I hope that ere long we shall meet for ever in God. Those who die are, in respect of us, but as absent for a few years, it may be only months.... God never strikes but in love, nor takes away save to give again. I pray Him to comfort you, to preserve your health, and to turn your heart wholly to Himself.

Blessed is he who lives in faith, trusts to none save God, and uses this world as though he were already beyond it.

On the thought of death

I cannot too strongly deprecate the blindness of most men for persisting in rejecting the thought of death, and turning away from an inevitable event which may be made most blessed by dwelling upon it. Death only alarms the carnal mind: "Perfect love casteth out fear." It is not because one imagines one's self righteous that one ceases to be afraid, but because one loves and resigns one's self unreservedly to Him Whom one loves. This makes death easy and precious. To him who is dead bodily death is but the consummation of the work of grace.

Men shun the thought of death as sad, but death will only be sad to those who have not thought of it. It must come sooner or later, and then he who has refused to see the truth in life will be forced to face it in death. Death brings a very clear insight as to all a man has done and all he ought to have done; we shall then see clearly how we ought to have used past grace, talents, wealth, health, time, and all the joys and sorrows of life. The thought of death is the best check we can put on all our plans and doings. It is right to wish for it, but we must wait for death with the same absolute submission to God's Will as we accept life. It is right to wish for death, inasmuch as it is the consummation of our repentance, the entrance to blessedness, and our eternal reward. A man has no right to say that he wishes to live to do penance for past sins—death is the fullest of penances; our sins will be expiated in death better than by any other penance. It will be as precious to the good as it will be terrible to the wicked. We ask for death daily in the "Our Father". Every one must ask that the Kingdom of God may come to him. So saying, we must wish for it; for prayer is the heart's desire, and God's Kingdom can only come to us through our death. St Paul bids Christians "comfort one another" with the thought of death.

(*The Spiritual Letters of Archbishop Fénelon: Letters to Men*, translated by H. L. Sidney Lear, Longmans, 1894)

PÈRE de CAUSSADE, s.j.

To Sister M. Antoinette De Mahuet   *1742*

... Though my health is consistently good, I am conscious that the swift passing years bring us nearer to that eternity to which we all must come. Admittedly this reflection is distasteful to our humanity. Yet, do we but regard it as beneficial, it becomes pleasant rather than otherwise, much as a disagreeable medicine gradually loses its repulsiveness as we grow aware of its efficacy.

... [I] perceive myself upon the bank, with embarkation immediately ahead of me. It is time, then, I must say with St Francis de Sales and Fr Surin, to make ready my little provision for eternity.... Nothing will comfort us so much in death as our humble submission to the various plans of Divine Providence, despite the insidious promptings of self-love that so often come under the most spiritual guises and with most plaudible pretexts.

ST FRANCIS de SALES

In the first moments of our bereavement we should endeavour to keep ourselves calm and free from thoughts of bitterness.... I would not, however, say, "Do not weep". No! for tears are but the reasonable testimony of the tender affection we bear to the dead. In shedding them we shall be but following the example of Jesus, Who wept over his friend Lazarus. These outward signs of grief, however, must be in moderation; our tears should betray more compassion and tenderness than vain regret.

We should not grieve like those who live without a thought beyond this miserable life, forgetting that we are journeying on to an eternal home where, provided we live according to God's law, we shall one day for ever enjoy the company of those we love. We cannot entirely keep our poor heart from feeling the loss of those whose companionship was so agreeable to us; but we must hold fast our solemn resolution never to allow our wills to be separated from the divine Will.

To a lady, on the death of her father

My Dear Child,

I know that now you will suffer much through the loss you have sustained. God has called your father to Himself: He has delivered him from the evils of this miserable life in which whilst we live we are dying, and when we die we begin to live.

I would lead you for comfort to Jesus crucified, at the sight of whom your faith will be animated, and at whose feet you will find consolation. Since Christ has laid down His life for us, the death of those who, like your father, depart in the pale of the Church, and fortified by its Sacraments, is happy; and he who rejoices in the death of our Lord should never lament with bitterness for those whom He has purchased by His Blood, and made His own. I say to all who apply to me for guidance: "Lift up your hearts" as the Church bids us do during the Holy Sacrifice . . . in saying it preserves a restful calm, I do not mean to imply that sorrow or affliction can find no entrance; no, my dear child, I would not say this; but I mean that together with the sufferings and tribulations which visit that soul, there is present a firm resolve to endure them for the love of God. And all their bitterness, how bitter soever they may be, is accepted in tranquillity and peace.

To a lady, on the death of her father

. . . As long as we lift up our eyes to contemplate God's providence, grief can have no power to hurt us. God and your guardian angel will have consoled you. I can add nothing. Your "exceeding bitterness is in peace". Of what use is it to say more? As God draws our beloved ones, one after another, to Himself, He draws our hearts with them. "Since I have no longer an earthly father," said St Francis, "I can say more truly, 'Our Father who art in heaven'." Often raise your mind, my dear child, to heaven.

(*Comfort for Mourners*, St Francis de Sales, translated by E. M. B. Richardson and Sons, 1879)

ANON

To a penitent   *Annecy, 7 April 1617*

I am seizing the earliest opportunity to write and fulfil my promise by laying before you a few thoughts which, if you reflect on them, may lessen that fear of death which terrifies you so much when you are ill or with child. Although the fear is in no way sinful, yet it is a pity, because your heart cannot be united to God in love so closely as it might be were it not so deeply agitated.

First of all, I assure you that if you persevere in a life of God's service, as I see you are doing, you will find that the apprehension will gradually calm down. Moreover, as your soul steers clear of harmful emotions and becomes ever more firmly fixed in God, you will notice yourself setting less value on this mortal existence and the stupid pleasure one takes in it. So go on steadily in the life of prayer you have begun, and advance daily from one step to the next along your present path. You will find that in a short time the terrors will diminish and no longer play such havoc with your feelings.

Secondly, often fill your mind with thoughts of the great gentleness and mercy with which God our Saviour welcomes souls at death, if they have spent their lives in trusting Him, and striven to serve and love Him, each according to his calling. O how good you are, Lord, to the upright of heart! (Ps. 72.1).

Thirdly, frequently lift up your heart towards our Redeemer in holy confidence mingled with profound humility, as if to say: I am wretched, Lord, but You will take my wretchedness and lay it in the bosom of Your mercy, and lead me by Your fatherly hand into the joy of Your inheritance. Weak, abject, and poor as I am, in that moment You will look on me with love, for I have hoped in You and desired to be all Yours.

Fourthly, do your utmost to arouse in yourself a love of heaven and the life of the blessed. Make it a subject of continual meditation. You will find a fair number of considerations set out in the "Introduction à la Vie devote", in the meditation on the glory of heaven and the choice of Paradise (Part I, Ch. 16,17): in proportion as you value and long for eternal happiness, so you will weaken your dread of parting from this mortal and fleeting life.

Fifthly, never read books or even passages in books which deal with death, judgement, and hell, because, thanks be to God, you have made a firm resolution to live a Christian life, and need no such incentives of fear and terror to goad you on.

Sixthly, often make acts of love to our Lady, the saints, and the holy angels. Make friends with them. Talk to them frequently, using words of praise and tenderness. When you have gained familiar access to the citizens of the heavenly Jerusalem above, you will grieve far less at bidding farewell to those of the mean city here below.

Seventhly, repeatedly adore, praise, and bless the most holy death of our crucified Lord, and place your confidence wholeheartedly in that merit of His which will win you a happy death—say over and over again: "O divine death of my sweet Jesus, you will bless mine and it shall be blessed. I bless you and you will bless me, O death more desirable than life." So it was that during his mortal illness St Charles had a picture of our Lord's burial hung where he could see it, together with the prayer on the Mount of Olives. In that critical moment St Charles wanted to strengthen himself by his Redeemer's Passion and Death.

Eighthly, occasionally recall that you are a daughter of the Catholic Church and rejoice in that fact, for the children of such a Mother will always die a happy death so long as they intend to live according to her laws. At the hour of death, so the blessed Mother Teresa says, it is the greatest consolation to die a "Daughter of Holy Church".

Ninthly, end all your prayers on a note of confidence. Say for instance: "O Lord, Thou art my refuge (Ps. 142.5): my soul trusteth in Thee (Ps. 57.1). O God, who has ever trusted in Thee and been put to shame? (Ecclus 2.11). In Thee, O Lord, have I hoped, and I shall never be confounded" (Ps. 31.1). When you make ejaculations during the day and when you receive the Blessed Sacrament, always speak words of love and trust in our Lord, such as: You, O Lord, are my Father. O God, You are the lover of my soul, the King of my heart, the Beloved of my being. O sweet Jesus, You are my dear master, my help, my refuge.

Tenthly, always look upon those you love most dearly and from whom it would be bitter grief to part as the very ones who will keep you company for all eternity in heaven—your husband, your tiny John, your father. "O darling little son, by God's help, he will enter one blessed day into life everlasting. There he will rejoice in my happiness and make merry, and I shall likewise rejoice in his and make merry, and nothing shall ever separate us more." Say the same of your husband, father, and so forth, and it will come the more readily to your lips, since your dear ones serve and fear God. You are inclined to depression, and therefore go to the "Introduction à la Vie devote" and see what I have to say about sadness and how to remedy it.

Here, my dear Madam, is all I can say for the moment on this subject. I have said it with a heart filled with tenderness towards you, and I beg you to give me a place in yours, and offer me up frequently before the divine mercy. In return, I shall never cease to petition that God may bestow on you His blessing.

Live happily and joyfully in God's love.

(To Any Christian, selected and arranged
by a Benedictine of Stanbrook, Burns Oates)

JOHN KEBLE

To a friend, on the death of his infant child   *1820*

My dearest——

It is presumptuous in me, I know, to pretend to comfort you on so sad an occasion as this, but I must tell you truly that my heart bleeds at the thought of your loss, though I know it is absolutely impossible for me to sympathise with you under it; but you have better comforters who do, not only—and dear—but a more effectual one than either, even Him Who when He saw a dead man carried out, the only son of his mother, had compassion on her. He is even now touched with a feeling of the sorrow of heart which has fallen upon you and your dear wife, whom God bless, confirm, and comfort for His sake.

. . . "For if we believe that Jesus died and rose again, even so them also which sleep in Jesus will God bring with Him." You need not look further for comfort than these words.

May He in Whom alone we can know comfort, make them, and all other consolations which His Providence has in store for you, so truly comfortable to you, that you shall be able to look backward, even to this sad time, with humble thankfulness to Him for helping you to suffer as Christians. So prays, from the bottom of his heart,

Your affectionate friend,
John Keble

To a father, on the death of his child

What can such an one as I am say to comfort a father at such a time as this must be to you that you do not know much better yourself? But in all grief it is something to see in a friend's handwriting that he is trying at least to sympathize with one, and of this you may be sure on my part. And whilst we are writing, and thinking, and trying, we are all, if we are not wanting to ourselves, coming nearer the perfect Comfort, of which all these are but shadows.

Surely as you have always been helped to feel for others, so many and many both here and there will be helped to feel and pray for you; and now we have the comfort of knowing ... that we may innocently and piously pray for our departed, and that they no doubt remember, and pray for us. Surely that one thing is worth a great deal of trouble and annoyance, such as seems from day to day to be gathering like a cloud around us.

On Prayer for the departed

I cannot doubt that He Who is the true Comforter has been and will be with you, tempering your loneliness with sweet thoughts, such as He only can impart, and that all that happens about your work and your dear children especially, will be providentially ordered to help and soothe you.

For one thing I will venture to send you a sort of suffrage, I believe from Bishop Andrewes, which one very unworthy person at least has used for years with far greater comfort than he deserves:

"Remember Thy servants and handmaidens which have departed hence in the Lord, especially—and all others to whom our remembrance is due; give them eternal rest and peace in Thy heavenly kingdom, and to us such a measure of communion with them as Thou knowest to be best for us. And bring us all to serve Thee in Thine eternal Kingdom, when Thou wilt, and as Thou wilt, only without shame or sin. Forgive my presumption and accept my prayers as Thou didst the prayers of Thine Ancient Church, through Jesus Christ Our Lord."

We think a great deal of you, my very dear friends ... but no doubt you are thought of there, where thoughts are deeds and deeds are blessings for ever. You must not be too disheartened, nor blame yourselves, if now at your first coming home, you do not feel so much alive as you would wish to the many blessings which are still spared even to your sight: it is a natural yearning which He Who spared not His own Body, nor His Mother's grief, will turn into a great grace for you all.

(*Letters of Spiritual Counsel and Guidance*, J. Keble, Mowbrays, 1920)

BISHOP EDWARD KING

To one who had lost his mother

Lincoln, 10 June 1887

I am so sorry for my delay in writing to you, not only about coming to you, as you kindly ask, but to assure you of my sincere sympathy with you in your great, great sorrow.

I wish I could come to you, but I am engaged to the full now, and I dare not add more. I was so grieved for you, and dear Reggie, when I heard of your terrible trouble. I know by experience how blank it makes things—no one to tell all the little things of interest to! No one to keep waiting for one and to help on one's self-planned plans! It is a terrible loss and blank. The point of unity in the family seems gone. But, dear friend, you will have help to bear it, and in time you will understand and see how all has been ordered in wisdom and in love.

Life never can be quite the same. But you would not wish to have it otherwise as you see the wisdom and the love which has ruled all.

A new nearness to God, a purer intention, a more direct living for the world beyond, a new freedom and sense of independence to the world, its frowns and smiles, and firmer courage; these, dear friend, are some of the gifts and consolation I believe you will find in God's good time. Meanwhile you can trust yourself to the prayers of the Church for those in "Trouble and sorrow".

My love and blessing to you and dear R.

Yours affectionately, . . .

To a friend, on the death of his married daughter

Lincoln, 17 January 1889

Thank you for your great kindness in allowing me so quickly to be with you in your great sorrow, for so it must be even to the most Christian heart. I had hoped, and prayed, that, if it pleased God, you might all be spared this great pain, but He Who did not withdraw the cup in the garden knows what is best. On this we may most surely rest, and in time, or in eternity, we shall know this. At present we may not be able to do more than accept and believe it, but such acceptance is surely most blessed in its fruits, for it is the union of our will with His Will, and this is a central point of the restoration of the divine likeness in us, and our especial preparation for our eternal communion in heaven. Through suffering we are perfected.

I am thankful to hear that you have all been sustained. I do not doubt that you will be, only I feel that the strain on the dear husband, and on dear Mrs V, and on you must be terrible. But I do not doubt He will sustain you.

I return (D.V.) to-morrow. You will have made your arrangements for Saturday, but anything I could do you know I shall be glad to do. I shall be engaged in the morning, but free in the afternoon. I only say this, not to intrude, but to assure you of my readiness to express my sincere sympathy in any way I can.

God bless you and support you all.

I am, yours very affectionately, . . .

To a lady, on the death of a sailor lad

Lincoln, 3 December 1889

Pardon my delay in returning these most interesting and precious letters. I have ventured to write a few unworthy words to poor Mrs H, if you think it well to send them. I am sure you must have suffered very much from this sad occurrence. But I am sure you may have the greatest comfort. This world is so full of difficulty and danger that one could not wish any back again who have been taken while on the right path. They have been saved we know not from what dangers of the young which might have ruined them.

It is very difficult not to be quite broken-hearted when such sorrows come, and life seems almost impossible at times; but He Who is the Life can support us, and He will. It must be, I am sure, a very great pleasure and satisfaction to you to feel that you did so much for the dear lad, and that he has won such a good testimony. I have, you may like to know, on more than one occasion spoken of the good lad's life and death in my Confirmation addresses; so that the seed is scattered for a wider and continuing life, and not really lost. Please God, in Paradise we may meet those whose prayers and early death have helped to bring us there.

May you, by God's blessing, one day join them, and then you will know that all your pain, and love, and sorrow were not in vain. . . .

To a friend—Dr Liddon's funeral

Lincoln, 19 September 1890

I must thank you—this I cannot really do—for all your most indulgent care of me. I am afraid I was very selfish and distracting in return, but it was a great pleasure and comfort to me, and especially at the last. It will always mark our little tour together! St Paul's was most wonderful. I never shall forget the effect of seeing the coffin carried from the choir down to the dome. It seemed to be floating on into a sea of living faces, which, in thousands, were gazing at it from every part of the great nave and dome. It looked like a foretaste of the welcome in Paradise. It was most beautiful. Good-bye! Please give my grateful thanks to your dear husband for all his loving care.

My love and blessing to you both.

On the death of Dean Church

London, 9 December 1890

The good and great Dean of St Paul's has gone, at least we cannot consult him as we used. It is very terrible. This last part of the pathway of one's life wants more courage and self-reliance than the earlier stages, where one had so many on either hand to consult. It teaches one terribly the folly of not living in the closest communion with God, the nothingness of popularity and human praise. Faith in Him and in His presence seem the only remedy against abject cowardice and flight. I have seen this more or less clearly all along, but the clouds of earthly things have left me more liable to fear than might have been.

What a beautiful life his was! So splendidly free from all this earthly dross and clouding; so pure, and, therefore, so strong. He seemed to combine the old Tractarian spirit of retirement with the highest and best modern culture and refinement. His wisdom and unostentatious knowledge were so wonderful.

His loss after dear Liddon's seems terrible. Perhaps it means that our natural strength is being reduced because God has some great victory to win for His Church, and may we not hinder it!

To a lady, on the death of his own sister

Old Palace, Lincoln, 29 July 1892

I must add a word of special thanks to you for your kind words of sympathy.

You have had so much sorrow that you know what it is.

I feel as if I had been in a storm, and my sails were split, but sail mending is apostolic work, and I trust that God will give me skill and power to make them strong enough (when, after a bit, I put out to sea again) to finish my course.

Sorrow has its strengthening side, has it not? It seems to take away the dross of the fear and love of the world. I hope it may be so, and that I may, if it please God, have strength to serve the diocese better than I have done.

With my love and blessing.

To one whose brother had been drowned at sea

Lincoln, 2 November 1892

Your terrible letter reached me last evening. I don't know what to say; it is beyond all words. Just not to be stunned or fall is as much as you can hope for for the present, then it will become a new power to you. Your life won't be quite the same. What people call a blow leaves a mark, but for good under God.

I will write to your dear mother. What it must be to them we cannot think! But He, Who gave His only Son, knows!

God bless you, my dearest child, and support you through this suffering, and rest, and enable others to rest more completely in His love.

Always yours most lovingly, . . .

To his cousin, on the death of her sister

29 April 1894

I have heard from Clevedon of your great loss and sorrow, and must write one word to assure you of my sincere sympathy. Dear A's life was one of great patience, but we must rejoice for her that now she has the full vision of Paradise without any veil between. May I say, dear cousin, how often I have expressed my admiration to my sisters at the way in which you have devoted your own life to take care of your dear sister? We all of our generation owe you a debt of gratitude for the example of unselfish devotion which you have set us. May He, Who only can, now be your stay and comfort! I am sure, after a little time, you will look back with thankfulness and comfort to the many years you have lived together, though it will be hard for you at first to know exactly what to do. There is a verse in the Psalms which has helped me sometimes: "I see that all things come to an end, but Thy Commandment is exceeding broad." In time you will see what His Will for you is, and then, I doubt not, find happiness in doing it again here on earth for a little longer, and then enjoy doing it for ever in heaven with those who have gone before.

May God bless and comfort you.

To one who had lost his father

18 September 1899

Thank you for your note.

I did not know that your dear father had been called away. It is a very unique epoch in one's life when that call comes, and life never seems quite the same after it. One loses the feeling of the safety of childhood, and seems thrust out into the cold. Yet it must be so, and we know it is God's own plan, and, therefore, the best. And, as you say, there are grounds for thankfulness that you have all been spared a long and painful watching. No doubt all is done well. R.I.P. I am sorry you cannot come for the Retreat. Would you like to come and stay with us for the Conference?

Please offer my sincere sympathy to your dear mother and sisters. God bless you and comfort you.

To a young man, on the death of his father

24 August 1901

I have seen in the papers what trouble you are in through the loss of your dear father, so I am venturing to write to assure you of my sincere sympathy.

I know by experience what a great event in one's life such a loss is—it seems to take away an old protection that one could feel safe under, and to push one out into the front, in the open as it were. I am sure you will feel it very much, dear man, not only for your own sake, but for the sake of your dear mother, for I think you told me she was living. The broken life of widowhood must be terrible; and yet the same Hand that made the two one can support them for a while apart, and then unite them together again for ever. May God uphold you all, dear friend, according to your different needs. He can, I know by experience, and I trust that He will. Then you will find that the withdrawal of this support will give you new strength, and though life will never look quite the same, yet you will feel that all is well done, and you will know the special sense of comfort and power that comes from Him as the God of the fatherless and widow. It will all help you to trust Him more and more. I am glad to think that you have the special love of one to comfort you. May God bless you both, and comfort you with the increasing consciousness of His presence and His love.

To a priest, on the death of his child

Old Palace, Lincoln, 7 April 1904

I am very glad of the opportunity of expressing to you my very sincere sympathy in your recent most sad loss. I must express my regret that I did not write at once, but you know how fully my time is occupied.

One great consolation we may have in the death of the young, that they are taken away from the evil and trials of this life to the brighter and far happier life above. For them we may indeed feel thankful, but that it makes another shadow on the path of those who are still following on here below. Yet shadows are made by sunlight above, and I trust that God in His loving care will give the comfort and strength to you and Mrs —— to follow bravely on till you meet again those who have gone before.

I am sorry to see that Mrs —— has been ill, and hope, please God, she may soon regain her strength.

Believe me, with sincere sympathy, . . .

To a lady, on the death of her brother

12 August 1905

Your kind letter telling me that your poor dear brother had passed away from us into the better world above has just reached me. I thank you very much for telling me. I was very anxious about him, and hoped he might have lived; but in truth he does live, and in a fuller and better life than we can live here. God often gives more than we ask or think. We asked life for him, and now God (we truly believe) has given him a long life, even for ever and ever.

But, of course, I know you must all feel sad at losing him, and his poor widow especially. Will you say a kind word to her from me, and give her my blessing, and may God comfort her and take care of her? He is the God of the fatherless and widow. And may God comfort you yourself, and his mother and brothers. Death is not the end of life, but rather the beginning of the higher and better part of life. The collect for Easter Eve speaks of death as a "gate"—"through the grave and gate of death", and I like to think of death as a garden gate leading into Paradise, which is the garden of God. There all is bright and happy, and we may trust it is so with your dear brother. He set us all a good example, and we must try and follow on and look forward to meeting again.

To the same, on the death of her father

Lincoln, 17 May 1909

How good of you to write!

I am sorry for you, and your dear mother; for your dear father we may indeed give thanks. It is far, far better to depart and to be with Him! Thank you for telling me of the beautiful example of his patience. We must try to follow on. It will be a great comfort to you that you have been able to help and comfort him so much at home, and your dear good husband too. My love to him. Give my love to your dear mother, and assure her of my prayers.

I shall always remember my happy visits to Hanthorpe; all will seem bewildering for a while. But in God's good time He will show you what He yet has for you to do. For the present, just trust to His mercy and rest in His love like a child. That is all we can do, and we may do it, and it is enough!

My love and blessing to you all.

To a friend, on the death of his mother

18 December 1905

Thank you for telling me of your dear mother's call to the better world. R.I.P. But you will feel the loss, I know. Life is never quite the same after such a loss. One feels left, and pushed on into the front, out in the cold; but it is the divinely appointed way in which we are gradually to sever from this life, and prepare for the next, which is the real abiding life. You have your own home comforts, D.G. They will shine out all the brighter and more comforting now. God bless you all and comfort you.

To one of his clergy, on the death of his wife

Lincoln, 31 December 1906

Thank you so much for telling me yourself.

I always think of you as one of my first friends in the diocese, and I shall like to think now of the same little churchyard with still more precious memories. One by one they seem to be gathered in, generation after generation. It is hard sometimes to work with spirit, knowing how soon the work will pass to other hands, but really the work is not ours. We are only labourers in His vineyard, so we must try to do a good day's work each day, day by day.

And you, dear brother, will find it, I fear, far harder to

have any heart for life; and yet He knows and feels for your sorrows, and can and will heal the broken-hearted, and give fresh gifts of faith and hope, so that you will have strength given you, I trust, and finish the work God prepared for you to do, and then will come reunion and rest.

That God may comfort and uphold you is the sincere prayer of yours very sincerely....

To a lady, on the death of her father, an old friend of the Bishop's

Upper House of Convocation, 3 February 1907

Thank you very much for writing to tell me, though your letter has indeed been a great shock and grief to me. I did not know that my dear old friend was ill. We were so much together at first, and though we never met but seldom of late years, yet he was always the same and the bond of real affection was never broken. You will, I am sure, miss him very much. Indeed, it becomes very hard to keep a brave and cheerful interest in life when so many are leaving us. We must be thankful for the comfort of their love, and try and look forward and upward to the life above. This life seems to be the place for making friendships. The next, we hope, will be for enjoying them. I am writing this in the midst of the discussions of Convocation, as I did not like to let the day pass without writing. I shall be with you in spirit to-morrow.

May God guide and support, and comfort you in your great loss.

To a friend, on the death of his wife

Old Palace, Lincoln, 9 February 1910

It is very kind of you to tell me yourself of your great sorrow and irreparable loss. May He, Who only can, support and comfort you. At first I can well believe the blow must be too crushing to allow us to do more than say "Thy Will be done". But in time, I hope, the brightness, and the wisdom, and love in which He ever acts, will appear through the darkness of the present cloud, and you will feel new strength to carry out the things that you have prayed over and planned together, so that your life will still have the consciousness of her presence helping you to persevere till you meet again.

That God may support and comfort you, and your family, is the sincere hope and prayer of yours sincerely, . . .

(Spiritual Letters of Edward King, D.D., edited by B. W. Randolph, Mowbrays, 1910)

E. B. PUSEY

On the death of a child   *1901*

No one but a mother who has had her last-born child taken from her, can know what the loss is. What any one can say is so on the surface. And they grate or seem unfeeling out of simple ignorance. Everything must seem very hopeless to you. It was to me, humanly speaking, when God took [my wife]. I dared neither look backward nor forward. I dared not look back to those eleven years of scarce earthly happiness. Onwards life looked so dreary, I could not bear to think of it.

. . . It seemed as if I was in deep water up to the chin, and a Hand was under my chin supporting it. I thought I could never smile again . . . many felt very lovingly for me; but it was too deep for sympathy. It was all on the surface, and the wound was deep down below . . . So I lived on, my real self sealed up, except when I had to sympathize with deep sorrow, and then I found that my letters were of use, just because I owned the human hopelessness.

Act day by day for the day. Thank God each day for all the blessings of the day, all the promise which you see in any of your children. . . . God teaches us by St Paul to be (*a*) "careful for nothing", (*b*) to "make our request known to God in everything"; but he adds (*c*) "with thanksgiving", and then he promises (*d*) "and the peace of God which passeth all understanding shall keep your hearts and minds". St Paul does not say it as a wish for them. It is an absolute promise. Do the one and God will do the other. All who have tried it have found it so. So many forget the "with thanksgiving". Take God at His Word and you will find it so. . . . What a great mystery life is! God sends us into the world, to form us amid life's daily nothings and trials for that character which we are to have throughout eternity; and every trial is like the blow of the statuary which makes the unshapen block take the form of beauty which He wills for it.

Sympathy   *11 November 1873*

. . . There is, alas, so little to be said! The Comforter alone can comfort. One only thing I know; I dared not look forward, not a day nor an hour. I neither dared look backwards nor forwards, but bound myself to the present instead. . . . I remember —— lying on her sofa, unable to move, recently a widow, with her nine children, so changed that I knew her only by her widow's cap; she said, "In the morning I know that God Who brought me to the morning will bring me to the evening, and in the evening that He Who has brought me to the evening will bring me to the morning." It struck me as so simple and so true.

(*Spiritual Letters*,
E. B. Pusey, Longmans, 1901)

FATHER CONGREVE, S.S.J.E.

To Miss H ——   *12 August 1908*

Death is no doubt coming nearer every minute to you as well as to me; but we will not allow ourselves to be frightened by the approach of death, as a heathen might be, as if death were an evil spectre coming to end him. Death, we will think of in the Truth, in God, as members of Christ. When childish pagan fancies about death scare us, as talking of ghosts scares children in the dark, we will quietly remember that death is Christ our Life coming to us; "The Master is come and calleth for thee" (John 11.28), opening the door for us out of the world of discipline into the world which is home, to change seeking and desiring into possessing, to change death into life which is life indeed.

When nervous fears present themselves, as they do to an invalid if a shadow crosses the floor, I would quietly go on with what I am about, treat the nerve flutter as nothing, look up to God and renew my confidence by some little act of trust. "Love is all, and death is naught."

The fear of not being in the faith when death comes, you can use against itself. When the fear suggests itself, take no notice of it but renew your act of faith and love: "Lord, I am Thine, O save me" (Ps. 119.94). The uneasy question arising, Am I safe? is not our fault, or our danger. The fault would be to surrender to distrustful questioning and fear; for that dishonours and grieves the infinite Love, who since He has given His life for you will not so easily let you be lost to Him.

Hope is not a little privilege given to favourites. Hope is a grace of the life of Christ given to every Christian in every sacrament, a grace like a seed, for the soul to plant, and cultivate, by acts of hope. . . .

I think the practical advice we want is to trust our Lord and give ourselves to Him, and distrust all nervous anxieties and reasonings that hide the fullness of the grace of His Sacrifice, and the mystery of His personal love and care for you. His way of leading you will not be His way of leading Mrs M or any one else. Be content to let Him lead you in His own way specially for you.

(*Spiritual Letters of Father Congreve, S.S.J.E.*, edited by W. H. Longridge, Mowbrays, 1928)

BISHOP HANDLEY MOULE

A letter of comfort to a sorrow-stricken friend

My dear Friend,

This is a letter from a stranger, for I do not know your name, nor where you live. But also it is a letter from a friend. We are friends, you and I, in more ways than one. We are beings with human hearts, and that is a true bond between us. Besides this, we are, both of us, people whose hearts have been wounded with great sorrow, and that makes indeed a strong and living bond.

MY SORROW

About a year and a half ago I lost my wife quite suddenly. She had been the light of my eyes, the strength of my life, for thirty-four happy years. One evening, without the least forewarning, in a few seconds, her spirit fled. Our kind doctor, when he hurried in, could only say, "She is gone". And thus I entered into the great shadow, into "the valley of the shadow", where I shall have to walk always now, till I die and go to see her again above.

I mention this grief of mine, not to talk more about it, but just to show you that I do know what a big sorrow is. So when I come, in this letter, to say a little about your sorrow, you will be sure that I feel for you with deep, tender, affectionate thoughts. And, oh, how much I long to bring you a real message about the love of the Lord!

YOUR SORROW

Well, I have told you of my sorrow. As to your sorrow, of course I do not know exactly what it is. But I do know that you have lost one who is very dear to you. And so your heart feels as if it had had a great piece cut out of it. You are stricken and broken in spirit. You are in a dark place in your life. Very possibly you are badly tempted to murmur, and to feel hard towards God. You are asking Him why He let it happen?

SORROW IS NOT SIN

First then, dear Friend, do not blame yourself for feeling your sorrow so deeply. Sorrow is not sin; it is nature. Almost the sweetest verse in the Bible is the shortest (John 11.35), "Jesus wept". He is not the least impatient with you for crying; no, nor for that deep sort of grief which would like to cry, but the tears will not come. Do not be in a hurry. Lay your tired head against your Lord and Saviour's faithful breast, and tell Him all. He is quite close to you. He loves you in your sorrow. He is moved tenderly towards you because of your sorrow.

THE LORD JESUS UNDERSTANDS IT

Remember next, that the Lord Jesus knows all about it in His own experience. He Himself has gone right through the most dreadful depths of grief. You know how He bore the great Agony in the Garden, and how He was tortured and slain on the terrible Cross; think of his holy body, a grown man's body, hanging by the nails for hours! And, you know how the sky then grew thick and gloomy, and how Christ's dear soul within Him felt a terrible "blackness of darkness". His body's awful sufferings never drew a cry from Him. But that tremendous woe of His soul forced Him to call aloud, "My God, my God, why hast Thou forsaken Me?" (Matt. 27.46). Dear Friend, this is all true; He really did endure all this great anguish, horror, and tribulation. To be sure, it happened long ago. But never, to all eternity, will the Lord Jesus forget it! Someone has said, "Suffering passes away; but to have suffered lasts for ever." That is a true saying. Wounds leave scars. Jesus carries the scars of His torture and His death always, in the very heavens.

And the joy of this, for us poor sinners in our sorrows, is that we have a Saviour who knows all about trouble! He can touch our broken hearts with a perfectly tender touch, for He has had a broken heart Himself. Let us thank and bless Him for His understanding love!

FAITH'S ANSWER TO OUR DOUBTS

Then, dear Friend, let me say a few words about that awful question, Why did He let this happen?

I have one simple answer for myself, when my own stricken heart asks, Why did He not save my dear one's life? The answer is this: "I do not know; but He knows; and I know Him!"

Have you a particularly dear and good friend, whom you entirely trust? And have you heard that he has done something very strange, very unexpected, so that you almost wonder if he has not done very wrong? But if you thoroughly know that he is thoroughly wise and good, you say, "I can't understand it; it is a great puzzle. But I do trust him, out and out. When I meet him, I am sure he will clear it all up." It is just so with the blessed Lord Jesus Christ, our Saviour and God. He allows strange and sad things to happen to us. But He has shown exactly what He is, how holy He is, how loving, how wise, how strong. Yes, he has indeed shown us this, by dying that awful death for us, and then rising again and conquering sin and death, and passing up in victory to the heavens. And now He just says, "Dear soul, I love you; I died to save you. Believe on Me for your salvation; come to me just as you are, to be forgiven and blessed; and then trust Me out and out—trust Me, most of all, in the dark. I will tell you all about it another day: but not to-day; before I tell you, trust Me."

A DREAM AND ITS LESSON

A Christian woman, a friend of mine, once had a dream, almost like a vision. She seemed to be freed from the body, and to be in heaven, amidst a circle of happy beings full of light and love. And then the Lord came to her, and she ventured to ask Him why there was such woe on earth while it was all so happy in Heaven above? He took her hand, and spoke one sentence to her. It was quite short, but it cleared up everything to her soul. She instantly saw how

God was Love in all things; she was too happy, almost, to bear it! When she woke she remembered all, except the words. So she still had to trust Him about the explanation! But she has remained always joyfully sure that all will be well in His time. Is there not a lesson in this beautiful dream?

THE SAVED SOUL'S HAPPINESS AFTER DEATH

Let me say a little here about the present happiness of the saved soul which is gone. Let us thankfully think what the Bible says about that bright life "within the veil". And let us remember that the Bible is the wonderful Book which our Saviour Himself loved and trusted, even in the hour of His death, and which he expounded to his followers after He was risen (Luke 24.27). Oh, how full the Bible is of glorious truths about saved souls when they have left the body! Think of texts like these: "To-day thou shalt be with Me in Paradise" (Luke 23.43). "To depart and to be with Christ is far better" (Phil. 1.23). When we Christians die, so we read, we are "absent from the body, present with the Lord" (2 Cor. 5.8). The Book makes us quite sure that the great joy of all joys after death is being wonderfully with the Lord Jesus Christ in His loving light and sweet glory, face to face. And also it assures us that the departed soul knows other dear and happy ones who have gone before, and is known by them. We are told that "They shall receive us into the everlasting habitations" (Luke 16.9). Yes, there shall be a grand welcome in to the Lord's own home; friends shall come to meet their friends at that door with joy!

Sweet shall the rest be there: "They rest from their labours" (Rev. 14.13). Loud shall the songs be there: "They sing a new song before the throne" (Rev. 14.3). Holy shall the life be there: "They are without fault" (Rev. 14.5). We may be sure that

> One sight of Jesus as He is
> Will strike all sin for ever dead.

They will always be growing in light and happiness there—but always altogether good.

RESURRECTION

Then, as we know, that blessed life has something more blessed still to follow it. For the day shall dawn at last when the Lord Jesus shall come again, "descending the sky", in all his shining beauty of majesty and love. Perhaps that day is quite near to us now, that day so great, so sweet, so glad. And then His buried ones shall rise. The dear, dear bodies that we loved so tenderly shall "be raised incorruptible" (1 Cor. 15.52). The grave shall hold its treasures no longer then. Your precious one shall not be forgotten then, but will arise, perfect in body as well as soul.

*　　*　　*

Shall not we who love our dear departed ones make quite sure of meeting them in that happy life of glory? Shall we not do so in the old Gospel manner? It is such a simple secret, but such a marvellous and mighty one!

> Just as I am, without one plea
> But that Thy blood was shed for me,
> And that thou bidst me come to Thee,
>   O Lamb of God, I come.

We have to let the dear Saviour have His way and will with us. We have to keep near Him, a day at a time, praying, listening to His voice, loving the fellowship of His Church. We have to let the Good Shepherd lead us. And He will lead us straight homeward, till we come, step by step, to the everlasting meeting again, in the holy glory, above all the clouds.

GOODBYE

And now I bid my friend an affectionate goodbye. We have talked together, heart to heart. I have seemed to sit with you by your fireside, trying to comfort your dear soul by thoughts about that blessed Lord Jesus who is all our salvation, all our hope, all our consolation, all our life, all our Heaven.

The puzzles and riddles of life and death are many. But He understands them all. We may think of them with blessed peace if only we come to Him, and look to Him, and trust Him.

I have an old book-marker, worked on pierced card; it belonged once to my mother. On the "wrong side" you see only a tangle of silk threads, all confusion. On the "right side" you see what the threads have worked out. It is those three wonderful words, large and clear:

God is Love.

In this life, my Friend, we see the "wrong side" of God's ways. In the life to come He will let His people see the glorious "right side". We shall understand then. We shall see then that the "stitches" which looked so wrong here were working out the right inscription all the while, to be read with joy for ever there in Heaven.

You shall yet thank Him, even for your tears. I have learned to do so. I find that my loss has taught me to comfort other sad hearts better, and that is a very real joy. So will your loss do with you, if you let your Lord help you to trust Him under it.

The Lord be with you! That is my best parting wish. If Jesus is at your side, you can say to the dear spirit that is gone:

> My loved one, I am not far from thee:
> Thou art with Jesus: He with me;
> And so, in deep reality,
> "Tis still together—I with thee!"

(This letter was written by Dr Handley Moule, Bishop of Durham, in 1916, to comfort those who had lost their relations and friends in the war)

BARON FRIEDRICH von HÜGEL

To a friend in his last illness

I hardly need assure you that your illness—the weakness and pain you are suffering, in their various degrees and kinds of tryingness—that all these things are now very much in my mind and heart. Indeed they remain constantly present before me, even when they have to be in the background of my consciousness.

With our dearest Gertrud we were able, for a considerable time, to hope that God would still give her many a year of life. And you yourself are not yet sixty, or barely that. May God give you yet many a year of life! But quite distinct from the question of the length of her life, was that of the *quality* of it—of the suffering and limitations mingling with, and imposed upon, pretty well all her activities. All these things were a present, indeed a pressing question.

And, looking back now, I am grateful for nothing so much as for this—that, given the suffering and trials which God then sent or permitted, He also soon gave her a light, far more vivid and continuous than it used to be, and an evergrowing acceptance and active utilization of it, as to the place, meaning, and unique fruitfulness of such suffering, thus met (as it were) halfway, in the mysterious, but most certain, most real scheme of the deepest life and of God.

When we first got to Rome she was wonderfully plucky and courageous, "grinning and bearing", a dear Stoic. But then gradually she became, in this too, more and more sensitively Christian. The Cross became, not simply a fact to bear somehow as patiently as we can, but a source and channel of help, of purification and of humble power—of a permanent deepening, widening, sweetening of the soul.

It was God's holy Will in *her* case that all this growth should promptly be for the other life. But it would, of course, in no way have been less precious had she been allowed to live on here, thus so greatly deepened and expanded, and rendered so far more helpful than ever before, and that for many a year.

I put all this to yourself, as I do to myself, because I have long felt that it is the *apparent sterility of suffering* which adds the final touch of trial to our pains; and that this appearance is most *truly* only an appearance. Not, of course, that suffering, simply of itself, is good or operates good; but that God is more living and real than all suffering and all sin; and that He can and will and does give concomitant opportunities and graces and growths to the sufferer, if and when the latter is humble, watchful, and prayerful in such utilizations.

How I wish I could help much, very much, to lessen your pains, but—I admit—above all, towards their transmutation! You can and will now help us all a hundred times more than when you were in health; suffering can be the noblest of all actions.

Your affectionately,
F. von Hügel

To the same friend

How wonderful it is, is it not, that literally only Christianity has taught us the true peace and function of suffering. The Stoics tried the hopeless little game of denying its objective reality, or of declaring it a good in itself (which it never is) and the Pessimists attempted to revel in it, as a food to their melancholy, and as something that can no more be transformed than it can be avoided or explained. But Christ came, and He did not really explain it; He did far more, He met it, willed it, transformed it, and He taught us how to do all this, or rather He Himself does it within us, if we do not hinder the all-healing hands.

Pray for us all, even just in passing, please. In suffering we are very near to God.

Your affectionate old friend,
F. von Hügel

To the same friend

I have your three letters—all written since I last wrote—all
before me; and I want, first of all, to say that you will never,
please, take any little delay in answering as the least index
of my feelings. I had to toil under much pressure until this
last Saturday afternoon—two days ago. And then a chill
drove me to bed and to sloppy food till lunch time to-day,
Monday.

But unless I am absolutely prevented by ill-health or
work that will not brook any break, I will write to you
every Monday late afternoon, unless (or until) you do not
find any special help in such frequent letters or for any other
reason which you need not ever specify. . . .

As to your spiritual question, my dear ——, as to how
you are not simply, once for all, at the beginning of all this
discomfort and pain, to accept and will it; but (as you most
rightly feel, a very different thing) how you are to stand it,
to keep on accepting it, day by day, even hour by hour,
possibly minute by minute (I mean as to the proximity of
pain to pain, and weakness to weakness): let me suggest to
you the following. I take it that this is *precisely the most
irreplaceable function and grace of suffering*, when it is at
all at its fullest, that we cannot, do what we will, cut a
decent figure in our own eyes; that it rises *emphatically*,
beyond a Stoic exercise. All we can then do (and how dear
and darling this poor little "all" is then to God!) is gently
to drop, gently to try to drop, all foresight whatsoever; to
treat the question how we are going to stand this for a
month, or a week, or a day, or even an hour, as a little
presumption on our part. We cannot really, of ourselves,
"stand" it properly, for half an hour; and God will and
does give us His grace to stand it for as long as ever He
chooses, provided we will, according to the intensity of the
trial, contract our outlook to the day, or the hour, or even
the minute. God, the essentially timeless, will thus and then

help His poor timeful creature to contract time to a point of most fruitful faith and love.

To the same friend

Of course I keep your case and its necessities and possible helps, well in my mind and in my prayers. And since you continue to press me, so gently yet so firmly, to propose to you whatsoever I may believe will or might help you to deepen your spiritual life and fully utilize the suffering that God Himself is now sending you, I will suggest the two following closer practices and self-examinations. I need not say that they are both intended simply as rough material, or approximate suggestions for your own experimenting and hewing into shape. I do not even want to hear your impression upon them—it all aims solely at the depth of your heart and conscience to help the fullest awakening and purification that God may call you to. Certain it is, that only such a growing, deepening (even if interiorly painful at first) can and will anchor your soul in a peace which not all the possible hurricanes of pain or oppressions of physical weakness can break you away from, really, at all.

I would then, first, get my imagination and reason into the habit, not simply of looking at, and looking for, sin as an offence against God, but of realizing and picturing it as *always* (except with hardened grave sinners) *chiefly a shirking of some effort, or loneliness or pain, etc., attached to a light of commandment as it offered itself to us, or a seeking of some pleasure, relaxation, vanity, etc., attached to the contrary course.* Now the cure—the only cure—for such shirking of right pain and for such seeking of wrong pleasure, is precisely the recovering (more and more deliberately) of what mean shirking and mean seeking. *Pain*—most real pain, which comes ready to our hand for turning into *right* pain—gets offered us by God. Try more and more *at the moment itself*, without any delay or evasion, without any fixed form, as simply, as spontaneously as possible, to cry out to God, to Christ our Lord, in any way that comes most handy, and the more variously the better. "Oh! Oh! this is real: Oh! deign to accept it, as a little real atonement for real sin!" "Oh, help me to move on, from finding pain so real, to discovering sin to be far more real." "Oh may this pang deepen me, may it help to make me real, real— really humble, really loving, really ready to live or die with my soul in Thy hands." . . . and so on, and so on. You could end by such ejaculations costing your *brain* practically nothing. The all-important point is, to make them *at the time* and *with the pain* well mixed up into the prayer. . . . Pray for me too, I beg of you.

Your very affectionate friend,

H.

(*Spiritual Counsels and Letters of Baron Friedrich Von Hügel* edited by D. V. Steer, Darton, Longman & Todd, 1964)

DOM JOHN CHAPMAN o.s.b.

To a Benedictine Nun   *25 May 1919*

. . . You ask why you are afraid of death. It is only human. St Teresa describes her mental and even bodily sufferings, caused by her violent desire to die and to "be with Christ". And yet, she says, she still had the human fear of death. And our Lord chose to suffer this fear of death for our sakes. The separation of body and soul is a wrench. On the other hand, I know quite well what you mean about the feeling— when you try to realize death—that there is nothing beyond.

The reason is plainly because *one cannot imagine it.* One tries to *imagine* a pure spiritual imagination of the soul without the body; and naturally one imagines a blank. And then one feels: "There is no life after death"; and then one says to oneself: "I am doubting the faith, I am sinning against faith."

All the time, one is only unreasonable—trying to imagine what can be intellectually conceived, but not pictured.

It is different, I think, if you think of death naturally; not unnaturally.

1. To die is a violence (as I said) from one point of view; but from another, it is *natural*. And to most people it seems natural to die, when they are dying. Consequently it is easy to imagine yourself on your sick bed, very weak, and faintly hearing prayers around you, and receiving the Sacraments, and gently losing consciousness, and sleeping in God's arms. (This is actually the way death comes to most people— quite easily and pleasantly.) And looked at in this way, it does not *feel* like an extinction, the going out of a candle; it seems, on the contrary, impossible to feel that this is the end of one's personality. But what comes next? We leave that to God—we do not try to imagine it.

2. Only in prayer can you get near it—if the world ever falls away, and leaves you in infinity—which you can only describe as nothingness, though it is everything.

The moral of all this is—do not try to *imagine* "after death", for imagination is only of material and sensible things. Only try to realize what it is to be with God.

One's *terror* of death, after seeing a dead person, is merely because it is unaccustomed. If you were an Undertaker, you wouldn't feel it! Nor even if you were a Nurse in a hospital. It is the thing to laugh yourself out of. But it does not matter much. Some people are afraid of mice or frogs. Some people are afraid of corpses. Some people are afraid of ghosts. Others can't stand the sight of blood . . . It is all a matter of habit . . .

These are gruesome subjects! I think it is much better to be accustomed to them, and to take them as a matter of course. The worst of death is really the blanks it leaves in this world. But it often fills up blanks in the next world; and we must rejoice when someone, dear to us, takes the place prepared "from the foundation of the world", as our Lord tells us, for that soul (at least He says "kingdom", not "place", I am misquoting).

To the same   *28 February 1929*

Please accept our sympathy in the loss of Sister ——. I have asked for prayers for her soul. . . . Don't worry about death. Usually when people come to die, they are either unconscious, or else quite peaceful, feeling it perfectly natural to die. But when we are *well*, it is naturally repugnant to us . . . always turn back and say: "I *do* want God, and only God; and death is the way to God."

> (*The Spiritual Letters of Dom John Chapman, O.S.B.,*
> *Fourth Abbot of Downside,*
> edited by Dom Roger Hudleston, o.s.b., Sheed and Ward, 1934)

FORBES ROBINSON

To E.N.L.

I do feel for you and could do a great deal to help you. I can only tell you what I have felt to be the only thing which makes life endurable at a time of real sorrow—God Himself. He comes unutterably near in trouble. In fact, one scarcely knows He exists until one loves or sorrows. There is no "getting over" sorrow. I hate the idea. But there is a "getting into" sorrow and finding right in the heart of it the dearest of all human beings—the Man of Sorrows, a God. This may sound a commonplace but it is awfully real to me. I cling to God. I believe He exists. If He does not, I can explain nothing. If He does, all whom we love are safer with Him than with us. If we can only get nearer ourselves to God, we shall get nearer to those whom we love, for they too are in God.

We shall be one, ever more and more really one, the nearer and the liker we get to God. . . . My dear friend, words are poor comfort at a time like this, when we see into eternity. A Person is our only hope, and that Person is God. God often takes those whom He loves best home to Himself as soon as He can. In the process of their development they break through the bonds of space and time. He has taken your brother, but not taken him away from you. We are all in the same home—praying for, knowing, loving each other.... I believe in the communion of saints—I believe that those who began to know God here, and whom we call dead are not dead. They are just beginning to know us, because they see us as we are—they see us in God. They are with Jesus, and Jesus is a human being. Because they are with a human being, a man, *the* man, the Son of Man, they must, they do, take a deep interest in the affairs of the sons of men, and—may we not believe?—in us, whom they knew below.... These are truths which sorrow helps me to make my own. I pray that you may never never "get over" the sorrow, but get through it, into it, into the very heart of God.

To W.P.

I don't think things happen by chance. Indeed I am sure they do not. I have never felt so humbled to the earth. One sees one's life as a whole, when one is helpless and can do nothing, and the whole looks very poor and mean. It is like the judgement day—only with this grand exception, that life is not yet over, that the night has not yet come in which "no man can work", that you still have a chance to make the future better, more honest, more noble than the past. Then again, I learnt the utter and wonderful kindness of my friends. I felt so selfish and so surprised at the goodness they showed me. Again, I saw something of the mystery of pain. My own was so trivial compared with that which some others had to bear. Yet I had enough to startle me that such a fact should be permitted on earth at all. I don't suppose we can understand its meaning; but my consolation was that it is not necessarily a sign of God's displeasure—that the highest life was a life of suffering, that the Son of Man was a "Man of Sorrows". Everything seems to me to depend upon the way in which one takes the pain—if one voluntarily says "Thy kingdom come, Thy will be done", then one is entering into the highest life, and pain becomes a new method of serving and knowing God. But physical pain, if prolonged, is a terrible thing; and there is no time on a bed of sickness for praying or thinking much about God unless one is accustomed to do so in health. The needs of the poor body press in upon one. Death-bed repentances are realities, but I am inclined to think that they are very rare. It is terribly dangerous to defer being good until we are ill. Illness does not necessarily make us good.

I am afraid I was but a poor coward, and yet my faith did not utterly fail. God is the one hope for a man who is ill, and He is true to His word. He hides His face behind the clouds; but even when I couldn't see Him at all, I felt that He was there. Pray for me; at present I feel too weak to pray much for myself. I want—I do want—to be a better man, to help others nearer the kingdom. I want, when life is over, to have a better record to look back upon than I had in hospital.

To an Auckland "Brother" after Bishop Westcott's death

My thoughts are with you at this time. I am most thankful that you have been a year with that man of God, and have gained ideals and inspirations for work which will haunt you all your life long. In moments of weakness, at times "when your light is low", the memory of his strenuous, holy life will be a power making for self-discipline and righteousness. And it is more than a memory. For he taught us by word and deed that we are all one man, that those who have realized what it is to belong to the body here will enter more fully into its life there. "We feebly struggle, they in glory shine"—yet we are verily and indeed one. That thought is often a comfort to me. When I feel the contradictions and perplexities and weaknesses of my own life, I love to think that I am part of a whole—that I belong to the same body and share in the same spirit as some other man who is immeasurably my superior.

When one whom we have known and venerated on earth

passes to the eternal home, it seems more like home than it was before. It is peopled not only with countless saints of whom I have heard, but with one whom I have known and seen, and hope to see again. His prayers for us, his influence upon us there are more effective than they could have been here.

The great triumph of Christianity is to produce a few saints. They raise our ideal of humanity. They make us restless and discontented with our own lives, as long as they are lived on a lower plane. They speak to us in language more eloquent than words: "Come up higher."

(Forbes Robinson; Disciple of Love,
M. R. J. Manktelow, S.P.C.K. 1961)

FATHER S. C. HUGHSON, O.H.C.

To two English friends

My very dear M—— and A——

I can't tell you what a grief and shock your cablegram has been.... My heart does indeed go out to you with all the love and sympathy of which I am capable. I wish I could be with you. It is not that there is anything one can say, for words are such poor things to express what we feel most deeply. But, then, they are not necessary. Heart can call to heart like deep unto deep and no word is needed.

Dear little John—how lovely he was.... God gives us these dear ones; they are ties which bind us here for a time, and then they are transferred to heaven and bind fast our hearts to the feet of God. The thought of them still loving us, watching over us, waiting for us, in their place of perfect peace, stimulates us as nothing else can do to reach out after the highest and holiest. It is unthinkable that we should not live in such a way as to make sure that we will not disappoint them. There is no purgatory for these Holy Innocents. They rest in the heart of God and their love impels them to pray for us; and there can be no more perfect prayer

than that which comes from the heart of a little child in
that blessed place. Is it not sweet to think of dear little John
praying for us all? The Church teaches us that when one is
given the vision of God in heaven, instantly every moral,
spiritual, and intellectual power is raised to perfection of
development. We wander through life so blind; even where
our intention and purpose is purest. We blunder along not
knowing what we should pray for as we ought. Not so with
the souls of the Blessed. They know; they have the un-
dimmed vision. All things are open to them. And this must
be peculiarly so with little children whose hearts have never
known the darkening touch of sin, with its blight on all the
faculties. I am so glad I baptized him. I am sure that because I did that blessed office for him, he will have some
special place in his little heart for me. That is a very happy
thought.

... I shall have you all in continual remembrance at the
altar. Give my love to all my friends. God keep you. "Underneath are the everlasting arms."

Affectionately in our dear Lord, ...

To a friend

My dear Daughter,

... Of course your letter did not get to me in time to
remember you and your dear husband on the 18th, but you
will both be remembered many times at the altar. God give
him rest, and may the Holy Spirit give you grace to go
straight forward in that way which leads to the great reunion in His kingdom. We need to recognize that death is
but an incident in the life of the Christian, a gateway, as it
were, along the road, opening into wider vistas of glory.
But the Communion of Saints gathers us all up into one
fellowship, and the great step into the life beyond seals that
communion as an eternally inviolable thing. ... You are
most right in the thought of our finding the closest bond
with those dear departed ones in our Communions, for
when our Lord prayed that where He was there also should

His servants be, I do not think He meant to confine that presence with Him to the heavenly places only; but if the prayer is fulfilled as we believe it is, wherever He is, there are they with Him. And so at no point of our earthly life are we in closer touch with these loved ones as when we kneel to receive Him with whom they dwell in blessed places. . . .

To one of his sisters, on the death of her husband

My dearest B——

I was much distressed when I came home to find the telegram about Jack. Dear Jack—God rest his dear soul—his gentle thoughtfulness, his kindly loving spirit which seemed never to put self first, but always was full of thought for others. If I, who saw him so seldom, was impressed with his character, how much more must it have been a factor in your life through all the years in which God gave him to you. I wish I could be with you to tell you all that is in my heart. I have been praying for you and for him and you may be sure there will be no cessation in my prayers.

We believe that he is in God's holy keeping and that it is only a matter of time when we shall all be reunited in God and find that joy which comes from the consciousness that never again will there be any separation, for that union is in and with God, which He promises to us who seek to be faithful to the light that is given. Only last night in the account of the raising of Lazarus I was reading of the tender, infinite sympathy of our Lord with those who grieve. The whole account, as St John gives it, is a marvellous revelation of the love of God for His people, a love which is to us a pledge that in the end all will be well if we continue to seek Him and His love and righteousness. He enters into our griefs and infirmities. He teaches us how to bear them and shows us that in the bearing of them we gain from Him ever more power and love, that in all these exigencies of life "underneath are the everlasting arms". His words to Martha have been an inexpressible comfort to millions of souls through all the ages and we find our comfort in them now. " I am the resurrection and the life; he that believeth in me though he were dead, yet shall he live, and whosoever liveth and believeth in me shall never die."

The passing from this life is not death; to those who have sought to follow Him it is an awakening to eternal life. We follow indeed so haltingly; there is so much that is not what we would wish it to be, but God is "full of compassion and mercy, long-suffering, plenteous in goodness and truth". That 86th psalm is so wonderfully filled with the assurance of His love, that we can rest on it in faith, letting nothing disturb us.

God keep you, my dearest child. Give my love to the girls and all the family.

Your loving brother, ...

... Yes, I shall certainly miss my dear old friend very much. This coming autumn will mark the completion of fifty years of our friendship. It is not often that one is given the privilege of such a long association. But as one goes on through life and sees so many pass on to the other side, there comes the ever-deepening realization that the gulf is neither wide nor deep between the souls at rest and those still in their pilgrimage. One is just a little further along the way than others, but they are all in the same way and all "in Christ". There can be no separation there. Death is not the close of one life and the beginning of another. It is only another stage of the same life, the further flowering of the life which is being lived under the guidance of the Blessed Spirit. One cannot fail to feel strongly the incentive to live well that we may not disappoint these blessed ones of their hope of seeing us again where they wait for us in their place of repose. Pray for his soul, although I cannot think that one with so loving a spirit which embraced everyone in its range so lovingly, will be far from the vision of God.

... In the old days people used to pray regularly for a good death, asking the dear Lord to hold them fast at the end. There are not many of us now who can say with the confidence of St Paul, "I have fought a good fight, I have finished my course, I have kept the faith". God grant that we may be able to say that at the last. But, after all, this life at its very best would be a poor thing if this was all there was to it. This world has nothing to offer except that which will vanish in a brief time, But God offers that which will never pass away. I am sure we do not think enough about this, and do not have it in our prayers as we ought. It would be a great uplift if we thought more about heaven and the joys that wait us there. ...

I am glad you remembered the blessed assurance—"The eternal God is my refuge, and underneath are the everlasting arms". You will find the passage in the 33rd chapter of Deuteronomy, being a part of the blessing which Moses gave to the people of Israel before he went up into the mountain to be seen of them no more. It is one of the most beautiful chapters in the Old Testament, and very full of comfort as it shows us the loving kind of God we have for our Father. That particular verse was called to my attention when I was a very young man, and I remember thinking that I should like to hear a sermon on it; but I do not remember that I have ever preached one on it, although it has been one of my best-loved texts, and I have used it many times just as I did when I called your attention to it. Nothing in all the Bible gives greater comfort. I am afraid we do not appreciate the Old Testament as we ought. It is much neglected, but nothing can be finer, for it comes through the inspiration of the Holy Spirit, and that is the assurance that it is full of love and strength. We should read and ponder it. Our fathers used to do this, but the Scriptures are much neglected in our godless age.

(The Spiritual Letters of Father Hughson, O.H.C., Mowbrays 1953)

ARCHBISHOP TEMPLE

LIFE AFTER DEATH

*To a business man who had consulted the Archbishop
on the "appearance" of his wife after her death*

Old Palace, Canterbury, 7 November 1942

Dear Mr ——

I am deeply touched tht you should consult me about this experience. I wish I felt more competent to help. I have always thought it a mistake to go into questions connected with spiritualism unless one could do it thoroughly; and for that I have had no time. But of course I have been interested and have reached some conclusions, which have, I regret to know, very inadequate bases. However, here they are:

1. I draw a sharp distinction between any experience which, like yours, is unsought, and anything resulting from resort to a medium or deliberate waiting for messages—e.g. by automatic writing; the latter so obviously makes opportunities for the subconscious mind to act.

2. So far as I have considered psychical phenomena, I know nothing that would persuade me accept so great a conclusion as survival of death if I did not believe it on other grounds; but as I do believe it on other grounds I am strongly inclined to interpret some of the phenomena as actual communication.

3. The evidence for appearances at the moment of death, or in a dream state at later times, of those who were very closely bound by love to the person concerned is stronger than for any other such communication.

With that background of thought I am led by the description of your own experience to believe that it was a perfectly real communion between you and your wife, in which she took the first step by "coming" to you. It cannot be more than a "probable" judgement; but the probability seems to me to lie on that side rather than on the side of hallucination. I think therefore that you should think it both possible and even probable that the experience was due to an external cause, and that God did thus permit your wife to make known to you her love and (so far as that might be called for) her forgiveness.

But all this rests on (a) faith in God and His care for us, (b) consequent faith in our survival of death and continued fellowship. And this order of priority is very important both for the logic of the belief reached and for the spiritual outlook of anyone who holds it. I was glad to see your phrase about God's permission to your wife to help you, because that shows that the right order of priority is in your mind.

Yours sincerely,
William Cantuar

To a vicar, on hearing that he was dying

Lambeth Palace S.E., 8 March 1943

My dear Cockin,

I have heard what you are facing, and I know that you will face it with faith and patience. But I want you to know how much my heart and mind are with you. You will be very much in our prayers. God be with you—holding you close to Himself and giving you, in spite of all, His own peace.

What happy times we had in many meetings when we were both in the York diocese! They are not lost. They all live on in that spiritual fellowship which death cannot break.

Yours affectionately,
William Cantuar

(*Some Lambeth Letters*, edited by F. S. Temple, O.U.P. 1963)

REGINALD SOMERSET WARD

To a priest on the death of an infant daughter

It was with great sorrow that I heard to-day of the death of your child. The religion of Christ was always sincere and clear-sighted. He refused to obscure the fact that tragedy was tragedy; and wept at the grave of Lazarus. It must therefore be in the circumference of His love that we recognize our torn hearts when we part with a child who has held all that was best in us to feel.

The fact that He could weep over the death of a loved one when He knew that in so short a time He was going to supply the answer which made hope the sequel to every tragedy, even the tragedy of sin, surely shows that here in time and space, grief and hope can come to us side by side.

Thus I pray it may be with you and your wife.

It has been given to me to see our progress to God as a road divided in the middle by a low wall, which we call death. Whatever our age or stage of development, or relationship with other human beings, there is no real change involved in crossing the low wall. We simply continue in a parallel course with those who loved us in our development and relationship. I do not believe that God has altered one whit your responsibility or service for your child.

I do believe that she will grow side by side with you, in spirit, as she would have done on earth; and that your prayer and love will serve her development as they would have done on earth. There is nothing static about the other life.

The difficulty is that our spiritual sight is so little developed compared with our earthly sight. We cannot watch the development and growth as we could on earth. Yet much can be done by faith, by the realization that what we hope is true, and that we can train our minds and imaginations to think in terms of truths, even if they are pictured in earthly forms. The companionship which was given you,

you still have. The growth to which you look forward will still be yours to watch over and care for.

You will be much in my prayers at this time. What I have written I know to be true and I pray that you may be enabled to live in that truth and to find the answer to your tragedy.

(*Death and Those We Love*, Alix and George Reindorp, Mothers' Union Publication, 1964.)

BISHOP WALSHAM HOW

Death

Death is a mystery very full of awe, and yet very full of blessedness. We shall soon know it better; but meanwhile let us gaze calmly upon it; for assuredly the more we do so, the less of awe and the more of blessedness shall we see in it.

Even to the holiest, Death cannot lose all its awfulness. It must always be a very solemn thing to go forth alone into the unseen world. And if some little fear mingles with the thought, who will say God's saints can never fear? A deep repentance, a bright faith, a glowing love, may be in the soul, and yet it may tremble at the great mystery of Death. So we will not think that some fear is of necessity a sign of unfitness. Men of hardened hearts sometimes die without fear. Very true saints and penitents sometimes tremble to the last.

But it is true that the more we know of Death the less we shall tremble. Nay, the fear is only a part of our poor human weakness; for why should we fear and tremble? Human weakness has always been afraid whensoever an Angel has appeared to man. "Fear not", is the Angel's salutation. So with the Angel of Death. We tremble because it is the visit of a strange unearthly messenger. Yet, if we be Christ's, we need not fear. The visit is to bring us "good tidings of great joy"; for it is to call us away from pain and weakness and sin and sorrow to perfect rest and cloudless peace. The messenger comes from our dear and loving Lord. He sends for us. He bids us come home. He says, by His messenger, "To-day thou shalt be with Me in Paradise."

O blessed Death! Is this thy terror, that thou callest the weary to rest, the troubled to peace, the wanderer to his home?

Does it seem lonely to die, because the unseen world seems to our ignorance so dim, and vast, and far, and strange? Nay; we are forgetting who will be there. The spirit will not sail forth in loneliness to search in the spirit world for some familiar thing. True, it cannot take with it any companion from this world; but are there none whom it will meet in the world unseen? Nay; Paradise has more inhabitants than earth has. And there is a blessed company waiting to welcome the passing spirit on the other side of the veil. In a moment it will be with all that blessed company. Oh, what sights and sounds will then burst upon us? For we cannot doubt that there is in the spirit world something answering to sight and sound in this world. But whom shall we meet there?

First of all, God, who has loved us and adopted us as His children, and redeemed us and forgiven us, and sanctified us—God will be there. He is everywhere, but there we shall have new revelations of His Presence and His Love. If this were all we should not be alone on the eternal shore.

Then too, Jesus, our dear Lord, will be there. He too will in some special and very blessed manner make His Presence known to the saints in the world of spirits; for He said to the dying thief, "To-day thou shalt be *with Me* in Paradise." And His faithful Apostle speaks of his "desire to depart and to be *with Christ*". Will not *that* be "far better" than to stay here, labouring and sinning and suffering?

But are there none others to meet behind the veil? O who has not at the least some *one* loved and loving spirit waiting there—waiting for a blissful reunion—waiting to welcome the newly set free spirit to the joys of Paradise? Most of us have surely more than one such gone before us whom we hope to meet. Some of these are surely there—waiting for us, ready to welcome us, ready to make us feel as though we had come *home*, instead of gone into a strange land.

And then there will be the good and holy men and women we have so often heard and read—Abel and Noah and Abraham and Moses and Samuel and David and Elijah and all the saints of old; and St John the Baptist and the Blessed Mother of our Lord, and all the holy Apostles, and all the glorious Martyrs, and all the pious women, and all the mighty company of those who have lived and died in faith.

Yes; it will not be lonely to die; it will be to pass into a great and happy company—to part from a little band of mourners, and to enter into the glorious ranks of the saints in Paradise.

Then welcome Death! Welcome solemn messenger from our dear and loving Lord! Thou comest to call us away to joy and peace untold. Thou art but as the narrow stream which parts us from our promised land. Thou art but as the little golden gate which opens into Paradise.

Pastor in Parochia

H. P. LIDDON

The first five minutes after death

Then shall I know, even as I am known (1. Cor. 13.12).

An Indian officer, who in his time had seen a great deal of service, and had taken part in more than one of those decisive struggles by which the British authority was finally established in the East Indies, had returned to end his days in this country, and was talking with his friends about the most striking experiences of his professional career. They led him, by their sympathy and their questions, to travel in memory through a long series of years; and as he described skirmishes, battles, sieges, personal encounters, hair-breadth escapes, the outbreak of the mutiny and its suppression, reverses, victories—all the swift alterations of anxiety and hope which a man must know who is entrusted with command, and is before the enemy—their interest in his story, as was natural, became keener and more exacting. At last he paused with the observation, "I expect to see something much more remarkable than anything I have been describing." As he was some seventy years of age, and was understood to have retired from active service, his listeners failed to catch his meaning. There was a pause; and then he said in an undertone, "I mean in the first five minutes after death."

"The first five minutes after death!" Surely the expression is worth remembering, if only as that of a man to whom the life to come was evidently a great and solemn reality. "The first five minutes." If we may employ for the moment when speaking of eternity standards of measurement which belong to time, it is at least conceivable that, after the lapse of some thousands or tens of thousands of years, we shall have lost all sense of a succession in events; that existence will have come to seem to be only a never-ceasing present; an unbegun and unending now. It is, I say, at least conceivable that this will be so; but can we suppose that at the moment of our entrance on that new and wonderful world we shall already think and feel as if we had always been there, or had been there, at least, for ages?

There is, no doubt, an impression sometimes to be met with that death is followed by a state of unconsciousness.

> If sleep and death be truly one,
> And every spirit's folded bloom,
> Through all its intervital gloom,
> In some long trance should slumber on,
>
> Unconscious of the sliding hour,
> Bare of the body, might it last,
> And all the traces of the past
> Be all the colour of the flower.

But that is a supposition which is less due to the exigencies of reason than to the sensitiveness of imagination. The imagination recoils from the task of anticipating a moment so full of awe and wonder as must be that of the introduction of a conscious spirit to the invisible world. And, accordingly, the reason essays to persuade itself, if it can, that life after death will not be conscious life, although it is difficult to recognize a single reason why, if life, properly speaking, survives at all, it should forfeit consciousness. Certainly the life of the souls under the heavenly altar, who intercede perpetually with God for the approach of the Last Judgement, is not an unconscious life. Certainly the paradise which our Lord promised to the dying thief cannot be reasonably imagined to have been a moral and mental slumber, any more than can those unembodied ministers of God who do His pleasure, who are sent forth to minister to them that are the heirs of salvation, be supposed to reach a condition no higher than that which is produced by chloroform. No, this supposition of an unconscious state after death is a discovery, not of Revelation, not of reason, but of desire; of a strong desire on the one hand to keep a hold on immortality, and on the other to escape the risks which immortality may involve. It cannot be doubted that consciousness—if not retained to the last in the act of dying, if suspended by sleep, or by physical disease, or by derangement—must be recovered as soon as the act of death is completed, with the removal of the cause which suspended it. Should this be the case, the soul will enter upon another life with the habits of thought which belong to time still clinging to it; they will be unlearnt gradually, if at all, in the after-ages of existence. And, assuredly, the first sense of being in another world must be overwhelming. Imagination can, indeed, form no worthy estimate of it; but we may do well to try to think of it as best we can, since it is at least one of the approaches to the great and awful subject which should be before our thoughts at this time of the year, namely, the second coming of Jesus Christ to Judgement. And here the Apostle comes to our assistance with his anticipation of the future life, as a life of enormously enhanced knowledge: "Then shall I know, even as also I am known."

He is thinking, no doubt, of that life as a whole, and not of the first entrance on it, immediately after death. No doubt, also, he is thinking of the high privileges of the blessed, whose knowledge, we may presume to say, with some great teachers of the Church, will be thus vast and comprehensive because they will see all things in God, as in the ocean of truth. But it cannot be supposed that an increase of knowledge after death will be altogether confined to the blessed. The change itself must bring with it the experience which is inseparable from a new mode of existence: it must unveil secrets; it must discover vast tracts of fact and thought for every one of the sons of men. Let us try to keep it before our minds, reverently and earnestly, for a few minutes; and let us ask ourselves, accordingly, what will be the most startling additions to our existing knowledge at our first entrance on the world to come.

1

First, then, at our entrance on another state of being, we shall know what it is to exist under entirely new conditions. Here we are bound up—we hardly suspect, perhaps, how intimately—in thought and affection, with the persons and objects around us. They influence us subtly and powerfully in a thousand ways; in some cases they altogether shape the course of life. In every life, it has been truly said, much more is taken for granted than is ever noticed. The mind is eagerly directed to the few persons and subjects which affection or interest force prominently upon its notice; it gazes inertly at all the rest. As we say, it does not take them in until some incident arises which forces them one by one into view. A boy never knows what his home was worth until he has gone for the first time to school; and then he misses, and as he misses he eagerly recollects and realizes, all that he has left behind him. Who of us that has experienced it can ever forget those first hours at school after leaving home; that moment when the partings were over, and the carriage drove away from the door, and we heard the last of the wheels and of the horses as they went round the corner, and then turned to find ourselves in a new world, among strange faces and in strange scenes, and under a new and perhaps sterner government? Then for the first time, and at a distance from it, we found out what our home had been to us. It was more to us in memory than it had ever been while we were in it. All that we said, and heard, and had to do, and had to give up at school, presented a contrast which stimulated our memories of what had been the rule of home—of its large liberty, of its gentle looks and words, of its scenes and haunts, which had taken such a hold on our hearts without our knowing it. It was too much; we had to shrink away into some place where we could be alone, and recover ourselves as best we could before we were able to fall in with the ways of our new life. No doubt, in time, habit did its work; habit turned school, I will not say into a second home, but into a new and less agreeable kind of home. And as the years passed, we saw repeated again and again in the case of others that which we had experienced at first, and with a vividness that did not admit of repetition in ourselves.

This may enable us, in a certain sense, to understand what is in store for all of us at our entrance, by dying, into the unseen world. I do not, of course, mean that this life is our home, and that the future at all necessarily corresponds to school as being an endless banishment. God forbid! If we will only have it, the exact reverse of this shall be the case. But the parallel will so far hold good that at death we must experience a sense of strangeness to which nothing in this life has even approached. Not merely will the scene be new —to us as yet it is unimaginable; not merely will the beings around us—the shapes, forms, conditions of existence, be strange—they are as yet inconceivable; but we ourselves shall have undergone a change; a change so complete that we cannot here and now anticipate its full meaning. We shall exist, thinking and feeling, and exercising memory and will and understanding; but—without bodies. Think what that means. We are at present at home in the body; we have not yet learnt, by losing it, what the body is to us. The various activities of the soul are sorted out and appropriated by the several senses of the body, so that the soul's action from moment to moment is made easy, we may well conceive, by being thus distributed. What will it be to compress all that the senses now achieve separately into a single act; to see, but without eyes; to hear, but without these ears; to experience something purely supersensuous that shall answer to the grosser senses of taste and smell; and to see, hear, smell, and taste by a single movement of the spirit, combining all these separate modes of apprehension into one? What will it be to find ourselves with the old self, divested of this body which has clothed it since its first moment of existence; able to achieve, it may be so much, it may be so little; living on, but under conditions so totally new? This experience alone will add no little to our existing knowledge; and the addition will have been made in the first five minutes after death.

2

And the entrance on the next world must bring with it a knowledge of God such as is impossible in this life. In this life many men talk of God, and some men think much and deeply about Him. But here men do not attain to that sort of direct knowledge of God which the Bible calls "sight". We do not see a human soul. The soul makes itself felt in conduct, in conversation, in the lines of the countenance; although these often enough mislead us. The soul speaks through the eye, which misleads us less often. That is to say, we know that the soul is there, and we detect something of its character and power and drift. We do not see it. In the same way we feel God present in nature, whether in its awe or its beauty; and in human history, whether in its justice of its weird mysteriousness; and in the life of a good man, or the circumstances of a generous or noble act. Most of all we feel Him near when conscience, His inward messenger, speaks plainly and decisively to us. Conscience, that invisible prophet, surely appeals to and implies a law, and a law implies a legislator. But we do not see Him. "No man hath seen God at any time"; even "the only-begotten Son, Which is in the bosom of the Father", is only said to have "declared Him", since in Him the Godhead was veiled from earthly sight by that mantle of Flesh and Blood which, together with a Human Soul, He assumed in time. Certainly great servants of God have been said to see Him even in this life. Thus Job: "I have heard of Thee with the hearing of the ear, but now mine eye seeth Thee." Thus David: "As for me, I shall behold Thy Presence in righteousness." Thus Isaiah "beheld", while the glory of the Lord filled the Temple. Thus St John, when he saw the Risen Saviour in His glory, fell at His feet as dead. These are either preternatural anticipations of the future life vouchsafed to exceptionally good men, or they are, as with Job, cases in which men are said to see God only in a relative sense. Sight does not mean anything spiritual which corresponds fully to the action of the bodily eye, but only a much higher degree of perception than had been possible in a lower spiritual state. Of the children of men in this mortal state, the rule holds good that no one hath seen God at any time.

But after death there will be a change. It is said of our Lord's glorified Manhood, united as it is for ever to the Person of the Eternal Son, that "every eye shall see Him, and they also which pierced Him". Even the lost will then understand much more of what God is to the universe and to themselves, although they are for ever excluded from the direct Vision of God. And they, too, will surely see God, who are waiting for the full glories of the sight to be vouchsafed to them after an intermediate time of discipline and training in the state which Scripture calls paradise. The spirit of man, we cannot doubt, will be much more conscious of the spirits around it, and of the Father of spirits, than was possible while it was encased in the body. God will no longer be to it a mere abstraction, a First Cause, a First Intelligence, a Supreme Morality, the Absolute, the Self-Existent, the Unconditioned Being. He will no longer reveal Himself to the strained tension of human thought, as one by one His Attributes are weighed, and balanced, and reconciled, and apportioned, after such poor fashion and measure as is possible for the finite mind when dealing with the infinite. None of us will any more play with phrases about Him to which nothing is felt to correspond in thought or fact. He will be there, before us. We shall see Him as He is. His vast illimitable Life will present itself to the apprehension of our spirits as a clearly consistent whole; not as a complex problem to be painfully mastered by the effort of our understandings, but as a present, living, encompassing Being, Who inflicts Himself on the very sight of His adoring creatures. What will that first apprehension of God, under the new conditions of the other life, be? There are trustworthy accounts of men who have been utterly overcome at the first sight of a fellow-creature with whose name and work they had for long years associated great wisdom, or goodness, or ability; the first sight of the earthly Jerusalem has endowed more than one traveller with a perfectly new experience in the life of thought and feeling. What must not be the first direct sight of God, the Source of all beauty, of all wisdom, of all power, when the eye opens upon Him after death! "Thine eyes shall see the King in His beauty" were the words of warning as well as words of promise. What will it not be to see Him in those first few moments— God, the Eternal Love, God, the consuming Fire—as we shall see Him in the first five minutes after death!

3

Once more; at our entrance on another world we shall know our old selves as never before. The past will lie spread out before us, and we shall take a comprehensive survey of it.

Each man's life will be displayed to him as a river, which he traces from its source in a distant mountain till it mingles with the distant ocean. The course of that river lies, sometimes through dark forests which hide it from view, sometimes through sands or marshes in which it seems to lose itself. Here it forces a passage angrily between the precipitous rocks, there it glides gently through meadows which it makes green and fertile. At one while it might seem to be turning backwards out of pure caprice; at another to be parting, like a gay spendthrift, with half its volume of waters; while later on it receives contributory streams that restore its strength; and so it passes on, till the ebb and flow of the tides upon its bank tells that the end is near. What will not the retrospect be when, after death, we survey, for the first time, as with a bird's-eye view, the whole long range—the strange vicissitudes, the loss and gain, as we deem it, the failures and the triumphs of our earthly existence; when we measure it, as never before, in its completeness, now that it is at last over!

This, indeed, is the characteristic of the survey after death, that it will be complete.

> There no shade can last,
> In that deep dawn behind the tomb,
> But clear from marge to marge shall bloom
> The eternal landscape of the past.

That survey of life which is made by the dying is less than complete; it cannot include the closing scene of all. While there is life, there is room for recovery, and the hours which remain may be very different from those which have preceded.

It may be thought that to review life will take as long a time as to live it; but this notion betrays a very imperfect idea of the resource and capacity of the human soul. Under the pressure of great feeling, the soul lives with a rapidity and intensity which disturb all its usual relations to time; witness the reports which those who have nearly lost their lives by drowning have made of their mental experiences. It once happened to me to assist at the recovery of a man who nearly forfeited life while bathing. He had sunk the last time, and there was difficulty in getting him to land, and when he was landed, still greater difficulty in restoring him. Happily there was skilled assistance at hand. And so presently my friend recovered, not without much distress, first one and then another of the sensations and faculties of his bodily life. In describing his experience of what must have been the whole conscious side of the act of dying by drowning, he said that the time had seemed to him of very great duration; he had lost his standard of the worth of time. He had lived his whole past life over again; he had not epitomized it; he had repeated it, as it seemed to him, in detail and with the greatest deliberation. He had great difficulty in understanding that he had only been in the water for a few minutes. During these intenser moments of existence the life of the soul has no sort of relation to what we call time.

Yes, in entering another world we shall know what we have been in the past as never before; but we shall know also what we are. The soul, divested of the body, will see itself as never before; and it may be that it will see disfigurements and ulcers which the body, like a beautiful robe, had hitherto shrouded from the sight, and which are revealed in this life only by the shock of a great sorrow or of a great fall. There is a notion abroad—a notion which is welcomed because, whether true or not, it is very comfortable—that the soul will be so changed by death as to lose the disfigurements which it may have contracted through life; that the death-agony is a furnace, by being plunged into which the soul will burn out its stains; or that death involves such a shock as to break the continuity of our moral condition, though not of existence itself; and thus that, in changing worlds, we shall change our characters, and that moral evil will be buried with the body in the grave, while the soul escapes, purified by separation from its grosser companion, to the regions of holiness and peace.

Surely, brethren, this is an illusion which will not stand the test—we need not for the moment say of Christian truth, but—of reasonable reflection. It is a contradiction to all that we know about the character and mind of man, in which nothing is more remarkable than the intimate and enduring connection which subsists between its successive states or stages of development. Every one of us here present is now exactly what his past life has made him. Our present thoughts, feelings, mental habits, good and bad, are the effects of what we have done or left undone, of cherished impressions, of passions indulged, or repressed, of pursuits vigorously embraced or willingly abandoned. And as our past mental and spiritual history has made us what we are, so we are at this very moment making ourselves what we shall be. I do not forget that intervention of a higher force which we call "grace", and by which the direction of a life may be suddenly changed, as in St Paul's case at his conversion; although these great changes are often prepared for by a long preceding process, and are not so sudden as they seem. But we are speaking of the rule, and not of the exception. The rule is that men are in each stage of their existence what with or without God's supernatural grace they have made themselves in the preceding stages; and there is no reasonable ground for thinking that at death the influences of a whole lifetime will cease to operate upon character, and that, whatever those influences may have been, the soul will be purified by the shock of death. Why, I ask, should death have any such result? What is there in death to bring it about? Death is the dissolution of the bodily frame; of the limbs and organs through which the soul now acts. These organs are, no doubt, very closely connected with the soul, which strikes its roots into them and acts through them. But, although closely connected with the soul, they are distinct from it: thought, conscience, affection, will, are quite independent of the organs which are dissolved by death. And it is impossible to see why the soul should put on a new character simply because it lays aside for a while the instrument which it has employed during a term of years, any more than why a painter's right hand should forget its cunning because he has sold his easel, or why a murderer in fact should cease to be a murderer at heart because he has lost his dagger and cannot afford to replace it. True, at death, the ear, the eye, the hands, perish. But when they are destroyed in this life by an accident, does character change with them? The indulgence of the purely animal appetite may depend on the healthy condition of the organ; but the mental condition which permits, if it does not dictate, the indulgence remains unaffected. Principles of right action or their opposites outlive the faculties, as they outlive the opportunities for asserting themselves in act. The habit of thieving is not renounced because the right hand has been cut off; nor are sensual dispositions because the body is prostrate through illness; nor is evil curiosity because the eye is dim and the ear deaf. And when all the instruments through which in this life the soul has expressed itself, and which collectively make up the body, are laid aside by the emphatic act of death, the soul itself and all its characteristic thoughts and affections, will remain unaffected, since its life is independent of its bodily envelope as is the body's life of the clothes which we wear.

One Being there is Who knows us now, Who knows us perfectly, Who has always known us. When we die we shall for the first time know ourselves, even as also we are known. We shall not have to hear the Judge's sentence; we shall read it at a glance, whatever it be, in this new apprehension of what we are.

It may help us, then, to think from time to time of what will be our condition in the first five minutes after death. Like death itself, the solemnities which follow it must come to all of us. We know not when, or where, or how we shall enter on it; this only we know—that come it must. Those first five minutes, that first awakening to a new existence, with its infinite possibilities, will only be tolerable if we have indeed, with the hands of faith and love, laid hold on the Hope set before us, in the Person of Jesus Christ our Lord and Saviour; Who for us men and for our salvation took flesh, and was crucified, and rose from death, and ascended into heaven, and has pleaded incessantly at the right hand of the Father for us, the weak and erring children of the Fall. Without Him, a knowledge of that new world, of its infinite and awful Master, still more of ourselves as we really are, will indeed be terrifying. With him, we may trust that such knowledge will be more than bearable; we may think calmly even of that tremendous experience, if He, the Eternal God, is indeed our Refuge, and underneath are the Everlasting Arms.

(Advent in St Paul's,
H. P. Liddon, Longmans, 1899)

Appendix
Bibliography
Notes
Indexes

Appendix

WIDOWS' PENSIONS
Fact Sheet No. 8
YOU AND YOUR PENSION
POSITION

TWO Acts of Parliament determine your pension position. They are:

1. *Widows', Orphans' and Old Age Contributory Pensions Act, 1925*, which provided for small pensions for widows and orphans of insured men, but widows of uninsured men could not qualify for the pensions on their own personal insurance. (Not everyone was covered by this Act because not everyone was insured then.)

2. *National Insurance Act, 1946*, which came into force on 5 July 1948, under which there was universal compulsory insurance, those under the 1925 Act automatically transferring to the new Act. The significant point in this Act as it concerns widows is that it removed the right of widows to receive a permanent pension simply on account of their widowhood. The right to pension was based on age, whether or not there were dependent children, and the three years' marriage test, AND the EARNINGS RULE was introduced.

BROADLY SPEAKING, the following are the rules in force for widows other than War Widows and Industrial Widows.

NOTE: All widows' benefits at all stages are subject to minimum contribution conditions on the husband's insurance: (*a*) at least 156 contributions actually paid and (*b*) for full benefit a yearly average of at least fifty contributions paid or credited (e.g. for weeks of sickness); where the yearly average is between thirteen and forty-nine contributions, reduced benefits are payable; nothing can be paid if the average is less than thirteen contributions.

1. *The Widow's Allowance* is a special payment FOR THE FIRST THIRTEEN WEEKS of widowhood (the Ministry term this "resettlement benefit" and we call it "bereavement money"), for ALL widows under sixty (and some over that age).

Present rate: £4 15s. per week, with increases for dependent children.

The Earnings Rule is NOT applied to the Widow's Allowance. After these first thirteen weeks a widow will have:

No Pension if she is without dependent children and under fifty.

No Pension if she was married for less than three years and is without dependent children (see certain exceptions for second widowhoods);

No Pension if she is still under fifty when her Widowed Mother's Allowance ends. (Special arrangements ensure that the widow who gets no pension is assured of cover for sickness and unemployment benefit at once if she cannot work when the thirteen weeks' allowance or a Widowed Mother's Allowance ends, even though usually she would have paid no contributions herself during marriage.)

These three "no pension" groups must pay the full insurance stamp (the rate depending upon whether employed, self-employed, or not employed) till the age of sixty, when they can qualify for the Retirement Pension, i.e. they must retire to qualify.

Widows of Second Marriages: A woman who has been married more than once can, in *certain* circumstances, count the years of a former marriage or marriages in addition to the years of her last marriage towards the qualifying period of three years.

2. *The 10s. widow.* These were only created under the 1925 Act. No "10s. widows" as such are created by the 1946 Act, BUT the carry-over provisions continue the right to this 10s. pension. NOW a widow can have the 10s. pension for one of two reasons:

(*a*) EITHER she is under fifty when widowed or when Widowed Mother's Allowance ends (and so under the 1946 Act is not entitled to a pension as a widow), but if her husband nevertheless was insured under the earlier Act *at* 5.7.48 AND she was married before 5.7.48, she retains the 10s pension as of basic right,

(*b*) OR she would have been entitled to the full Widow's Pension, but, because of the level of her earnings her benefit is reduced to 10s. (see Earnings Rule).

3. *Widowed Mother's Allowance* is payable to widows with dependent children ("dependence" over the age of fifteen, the statutory school leaving age, is subject to certain conditions). This is made up of "personal allowance" for the mother and allowances for each child. The widow still draws the Family Allowance (i.e. none for the first child, 8s. for the second child, 10s. for third and subsequent children), and so the rate of the widow's child allowances take these Family Allowances into account. As a widow, for her first child she gets 30s. (that child does not qualify for Family Allowance); 22s. for her second child plus 8s. Family Allowance; third child 22s. plus Family Allowance of 10s.

PRESENT RATES OF WIDOWED MOTHER'S ALLOWANCE

		PROPOSED NEW RATES ON 30. 3. 64
Personal allowance for widow	£3 7s. 6d.	no change
Basic allowance for first child	£1 10s. 0d.	£1 17s. 6d.
,, ,, ,, second child	£1 2s. 0d.	£1 9s. 6d.
,, ,, ,, third child	£1 2s. 0d.	£1 7s. 6d.

NOTE: Although the widow may not have a child who qualifies for a child's increase (that is, the child has left school and is not a low wage apprentice), she can draw a Widowed Mother's

Allowance at the *personal* rate provided only that the child is under the age of eighteen (nineteen from 30.3.64) *and living with her.*

4. *The Widow's Pension* is payable to women over fifty when widowed, or when Widowed Mother's Allowance ends, provided three years have elapsed since the date of marriage.

Present rate: £3 7s. 6d. a week

At sixty the Widow's Pension will be changed to Retirement Pension (subject to retirement), the amount is the same. The chief advantage to the widow with this change at sixty will be to avail herself of the social service amenities, that may go with Retirement Pensions and not with Widows' Pensions, for example, cheap cinema seats, hair cuts, chiropody, meals and amenities at Old People's Centres; these vary very much according to the area.

5. *The Earnings Rule* is applied to *Widowed Mother's Allowance*, *Widow's Pension* and *Retirement Pension*. It is NOT applied to the *Widow's Allowance* (see Part 1), Industrial Widows' Pensions or War Widows' Pensions (see Parts 7 and 8). It is also not applied to the *basic* 10s. pension. It further does not apply to the *private income* of a widow (that adjustment is taken care of by taxation).

	PRESENT EARNINGS LIMITS	PROPOSED LIMITS 30. 3. 64
Widow's Pension, Retirement Pension	£4 5s. od.	£5
Widowed Mother's Allowance	£6 os. od.	£7

Any earnings above these limits will be reduced by 6d for each 1s. in the first 20s. over the limits, then by 1s. for each 1s. earned above the limits-plus-20s. In the case of the Widowed Mother's Allowance, it is only the *personal* part of her allowance that is affected (and that is never reduced below 26s.). Expenses incurred in the course of working (e.g. P.A.Y.E. income tax, travelling, overalls, child-minding, etc.) are allowed before arriving at the limit at which the Earnings Rule is applied.

Luncheon Vouchers and the money value of "free" board and lodging count as money earned—otherwise those receiving these would have allowances which others did not have before applying the Earnings Rule.

6. *How Claims Are Decided.* Claims for benefit are decided by independent authorities consisting of insurance officers, local tribunals, and National Insurance Commissioner (or Industrial Injuries Commissioner). Every claim is considered in the first place by an insurance officer. If you are not satisfied with his decision you may appeal to the local tribunal within twenty-one days. You have a further right of appeal (within three months of the tribunal's decision) to the National Insurance Commissioner (or Industrial Injuries Commissioner) appointed by the Crown.

7. *Industrial Widows* are widows whose husbands died as a result of an accident at work or a prescribed industrial disease and provided the husbands were insured under the Industrial Injuries Scheme. There is no condition as to the length of insurance or the number of contributions paid.

8. *War Widows* are women whose husbands died as a result of service in H.M. Forces, or whose husbands, being gainfully occupied civilians, died as a result of war injury, or whose husbands died as a direct result of war service injury as Civil Defence volunteers.

Special conditions relating to second widowhood

The three years' marriage test is the same as for first widowhood, BUT if a woman is widowed for a second time in a marriage of less than three years, and IF the gap between the death of the first husband and her re-marriage is less than three years, then the duration of the first marriage plus the duration of the second marriage may be counted for the qualifying period of three years. ALSO if she is widowed a second time within three years of the second marriage, and having remarried within less than three years of ceasing to have Widowed Mother's Allowance under the first marriage, then the duration of the first marriage and the period during which she drew Widowed Mother's Allowance count towards the three years' marriage test.

CRUSE CLUBS

Counselling Service for Widows and their Children.
The Charter House, Lion Gate Gardens, Richmond, Surrey.
Tel. RIC 2660

Bibliography

BOOKS

Agee, James. *A Death in The Family.* Avon Books 1963.

A. M. W. *The Threshold: Reflections on Death.* Constable 1923.

Anthony, Sylvia. *The Child's Discovery of Death.* Routledge & Kegan Paul 1940.

Armstrong, W. H. *Through Troubled Waters.* Harper 1957.

Augustine, St. *Confessions.* Nelson 1938.

Bachmann, C. C. *Ministering to the Grief Sufferer.* Prentice Hall 1964.

Barton, B. A. *As Love is Deep.* Gollancz 1958.

Belgum, D. *Why did it happen to me?* Augsburg Pub. 1960

Bowlby, J. *Child Care and the Growth of Love.* Pelican 1955.

Bowman, Leroy. *The American Funeral.* Public Affairs Press 1959.

Cabot, R. C. and Dicks, R. L. *The Art of Ministering to the Sick.* Macmillan 1936.

Cammaerts, Emile. *Upon This Rock.* Cresset 1942.

Caplan, Gerald. *An Approach to Community Mental Health.* Tavistock Publ. 1961.

Caussade, J. P. de. *Spiritual Letters.* Burns Oates 1934.

Chaloner, L. M. *Bereavement.* Delisle, London 1959.

Church, Leslie. *Yonder: A Little Book for the Bereaved.* Epworth Press 1962.

Cicero. *Tusculan Disputations.* Heinemann 1950.

Coburn, John. *Anne and the Sand Dobbies.* Seabury Press 1964.

Crosbie, M. W. *The Lamps still Burn.* Birmingham 1945.

Davey, Richard. *A History of Mourning.* Jays, Regent St 1889.

Dean, D. K. *To Those Who Mourn.* C. H. Book Room 1946.

Dicks, R. C. and Kepler, T. *And Peace at The Last.* Westminster 1953.

Doniger, Simon (ed.) *Bereavement—Death—The Funeral.* Pastoral Psychology Press, N.Y. 1955.

Doniger, Simon (ed.). *The Minister's Consultation Clinic.* Channel Press, Great Neck, N.Y. 1955.

Evelyn, Joan. *Widowhood.* Mowbray 1960.

Farrer, Austin. *Love Almighty and Ills Unlimited.* Collins 1962.

Feifel, H. (ed.). *The Meaning of Death.* McGraw Hill Book Co. 1959.

Fulton, Robert (ed.). *Death and Identity.* Wiley and Sons 1965.

Goldstein, Rabbi. *Mourner's Devotions.* New York 1941.

Gorer, Geoffrey. *Death, Grief and Mourning.* Cresset Press 1965.

G.M. *Comforting Words for Widows and Others who Mourn.* London 1905.

Griffith, Leonard. *Pathways to Happiness.* Independent Press 1964.

Gummer, Selwyn. *The Chavasse Twins.* Hodder and Stoughton 1963.

Hackel, Sergei. *One, of Great Price.* Darton, Longman and Todd 1965.

Hall, B. *The Mastery of Grief.* A. Melrose 1913.

Harton, Sibyl. *Doors of Eternity.* Hodder and Stoughton 1965.

Hudleston, Dom Roger. *The Spiritual Letters of Dom John Chapman.* Sheed and Ward 1954.

Ilg, F. and Ames, L. *Child Behaviour*: Dell Publ. N.Y. 1955.

Inge, W. R. *Personal Religion and the Life of Devotion.* Longmans 1924.

Irion, Paul. *The Funeral and the Mourners.* Abingdon Press 1954.

—— *The Funeral: Vestige or Value?* Abingdon Press 1966.

Jackson, E. *The Pastor and his People.* Channel Press 1963.

—— *Understanding Grief.* Abingdon Press 1957.

—— *You and Your Grief.* Channel Press 1961.

—— *Telling a Child about Death.* Channel Press 1965.

Jerome, St. *Select Letters.* Heinemann 1954.

Kean, C. D. *Christian Faith and Pastoral Care.* S.P.C.K. 1961.

Keble, John. *Letters of Spiritual Counsel and Guidance.* Mowbray 1920.

Lear, H. L. S. *The Spiritual Letters of Archbishop Fénelon.* Longmans 1894.

Leighton, A. H. (ed.). *Exploration in Social Psychiatry.* Basic Books 1957.

Lewis, C. S. *A Grief Observed.* Faber 1961.

—— *Surprised by Joy*. Fontana Books, Collins 1959.

—— *Letters to Malcolm*. Bles 1964.

Liebman, J. *Peace of Mind*. Heinemann 1946.

—— (ed.). *Psychiatry and Religion*. Beacon Press, Boston 1948.

Lilje, H. *The Valley of the Shadows*. S.C.M. Press 1950.

Linn and Schwartz. *Psychiatry and Religious Experience*. Random House 1958.

Longridge, W. H. (ed.). *Spiritual Letters of Father Congreve*. Mowbray 1928.

Mahon, P. G. *Your Bereavement*. Hodder and Stoughton 1958.

Manktelow, M. R. J. *Forbes Robinson: Disciple of Love*. S.P.C.K. 1961.

Marriot, E. *Lux in Tenebris*. London 1900.

Marris, P. *Widows and their Families*. Routledge and Kegan Paul 1958.

McEwen, John. *Fénelon Letters*. Harvill Press 1964.

Mitford, J. *The American Way of Death*. Gollancz 1963.

Moule, H. C. G. *Christus Consolator*. S.P.C.K. 1915.

Naylor, V. M. *Emotional Problems of Cancer Patients*. Kershaw Press 1964.

Northridge, W. L. *Disorders of the Emotional and Spiritual Life*. Allen and Unwin 1960.

Oates, Wayne. *Anxiety in Christian Experience*. Allen and Unwin 1958.

—— *The Christian Pastor*. Westminster Press 1951.

Philippe, A. *No Longer than a Sigh*. Michael Joseph 1964.

Phillips, W. H. *The Conquest of Death*. Compiler, Torquay 1944.

Plutarch. *Moralia II*. Heinemann 1956.

Pollock, B. *A Letter to Mourners*. S.P.C.K. 1930.

Post, L. van der. *Venture to the Interior*. Penguin 1957.

Pugsley, C. H. *In Sorrow's Lone Hour*. A. James 1964.

Pusey, E. B. *Spiritual Letters*. Longmans 1901.

Ramsey, A. M. *The Resurrection of Christ*. Fontana 1961.

Reindorp, A. & G. *Death and Those We Love*. Mothers' Union 1964.

Rogers, W. F. *Ye shall be Comforted*. Westminster Press 1950.

Sales, Francis de. *Comfort for Mourners*. Richardson and Son, London 1879.

Seneca. *Moral Essays II*. Heinemann 1958.

Sinker, J. *Through the Grave and Gate of Death*. Skeffington 1925.

Stark, J. *Comradeship in Sorrow*. Oliphant 1907.

Stephenson, J. C. *Praying for the Dead*. Church Union 1962.

Stride, S. *The Anatomie of Mortalitie*. 1616.

Tatlock, Richard. *In My Father's House*. Mowbray 1956.

Thurian, Max. *Modern Man and Spiritual Life*. Lutterworth Press 1963.

Torrie, M. *The Widow's Child*. Cruse Club. Publ. 1964.

Townsend, Peter. *The Family Life of Old People*. Pelican Book 1963.

Urch, E. *Be Still My Soul*. Arthur James 1964.

Vernon, E. T. *Where Grave Thy Victory?* St Andrew Press 1955.

Vries, Peter de. *The Blood of the Lamb*. Gollancz 1963.

Wand, Wm. *Changeful Page*. Hodder and Stoughton 1965.

Waugh, E. *The Loved One*. Penguin Books 1952.

Westberg, G. *Good Grief*. Fortress Press, Philadelphia 1962.

—— *Minister and Doctor Meet*. Harper 1961.

Williams, John G. *On the Death of a Child*. S.P.C.K. 1965.

Winnicott, D. W. *The Child, the Family and the Outside World*. Pelican Books 1964.

Wingate, W. (ed.). *Lux in Tenebris*. Stock, Exeter 1892.

Wise, Carroll. *Pastoral Counselling*. Harper 1951.

Wynn, M. *Fatherless Families*. Joseph 1964.

Young, Richard. *The Pastor's Hospital Ministry*. Broadman Press 1954.

Young, R. K. and Meiburg, A. L. *Spiritual Therapy*. Hodder and Stoughton 1960.

ARTICLES

Barry, H. "Signs of Maternal Bereavement before Age of Eight in Psychiatric Patients", *Archives of Neurology and Psychiatry* 62, 1949, pp. 630ff.

Becker, H. "The Sorrows of Bereavement", *Journal of Abnormal and Social Psychology* 27, 1933, pp. 391–410.

Becker and Hill. "Bereavement: Inevitable but not Insurmountable", *Family, Marriage, Parenthood*, Boston 1955.

Benda, C. "Bereavement and Grief Work", *Journal of Pastoral Care XVI*, Spring 1962, No. 1, pp. 1–13.

Best, Pauline. "An Experiment in Interpreting Death to Children", *Journal of Pastoral Care*, Spring 1948, pp. 29–34.

Block, S. L. "St Augustine on Grief and Other Psychological Matters", *American Journal of Psychiatry* 122, 8, 1966.

Bowlby, J. "Childhood Mourning and its Implications for Psychiatry", Adolph Meyer Lecture, *American Journal of Psychiatry* 118, 1961, pp. 481–98.

—— "Grief and Mourning in Infancy", *The Psychoanalytic Study of the Child* 15, 1960, pp. 9–52.

Brown, F. "Depression and Childhood Bereavement", *Journal of Mental Science* 107, 1961, pp. 754–77.

—— and others. "The Remote and Immediate Effects of Orphanhood", *Proceedings of 3rd World Congress of Psychiatry*, Montreal, June 1961.

Carr, Winifred (ed.). "When They Miss a Father Most", Kate Wharton, *Daily Telegraph*, 21 May 1965.

Carrington, W. L. "First Aid in Counselling: 1. The Bereaved", *The Expository Times*, November 1965, pp. 40–4.

Church Information Office. "The Disposal of Cremated Remains", *Council for the Care of Churches* 1965.

Cohen, J. "Loneliness", *Family Doctor*, December 1964.

Deutsch, H. "Absence of Grief", *Psychoanalytical Quarterly*, 6. 1937, pp. 12–22.

Eliot, T. D. "A Step Towards the Social Psychology of Bereavement". *Journal of Abnormal and Social Psychology*, Vol. 27, 1933, pp. 380–90.

Engel, G. L. "Grief and Grieving", *American Journal of Nursing*, September 1964, pp. 93ff.

Felix, R. H. "The Rôle of The Clergyman in Time of Crisis", Prepared for Conference on Pastoral Care, University of Florida, 22 October 1963.

Freud, Sigmund. "Mourning and Melancholia", *Collected Papers* Vol. IV, Hogarth Press 1948, pp. 152–70.

Gorer, G. "The British Way of Death", *Sunday Times Weekly Review*, 15 November 1964.

Klein, M. "Mourning and its Relation to Manic-Depressive States", *International Journal of Psychoanalysis* 21, 1940, pp. 125–53.

Letourneau, C. V. "A Soliloquy on Death", *Hospital Management* 1963, pp. 58–60.

Lindemann, E. "Symptomatology and Management of Acute Grief", *American Journal of Psychiatry*, September 1944, pp. 141–9.

Maurer, Adah. "Maturation of Concepts of Death", *British Journal of Medical Psychology* 39, 1966, pp. 35ff.

Parkes, C. M. "Effects of Bereavement on Physical and Mental Health", *British Medical Journal*, 1 August 1964, pp. 274f.

—— "Grief as an Illness", *New Society*, No. 80, 9 April 1964.

—— "Recent Bereavement as a Cause of Mental Illness", *British Journal of Psychiatry* 110, 1964, pp. 198–204.

Pentney, B. H. "Grief", *Nursing Times*, 13 November 1964, pp. 1496–8.

Pius, Pope. "The Greatness of Widowhood", International Family Days Conference.

Robertson, J. "Some Responses of Young Children to the Loss of Maternal Care", *Nursing Times*, 18 April 1953.

Stern, K. and others. "Grief Reactions in Later Life", *American Journal of Psychiatry* 108, 1951, pp. 289–94.

Sullings, J. F. "Consoling the Bereaved", *Guild of Catholic Psychiatrists' Bulletin*, Vol. IX, No. 4, October 1962.

Symposium, "Grief and Mourning", *Contact*, 12 October 1964.

Torrie, A. "Community Care of the Widow", *British Medical Journal*, 23 April 1960.

Young, Benjamin and Wallis. "The Mortality of Widows", *Lancet*, 31 August 1963, 2, pp. 454–6.

Notes to Part One

CHAPTER 1

1. Cicero, *Tusculan Disputations*, Loeb Classical Library, trans. J. E. King, Heinemann 1927. III, vi.

2. Cicero, *Letters to his Friends*, Loeb Classical Library, trans. W. G. Williams, Heinemann 1958. Letters V and XVI.

3. *Tusculan Disputations*, loc. cit.

4. Plutarch, *Selected Essays on Love, the Family and the Good Life*, trans. Moses Hadas, Mentor Book 1957, pp. 93–100.

5. Plutarch, *Moralia*, Vol II, Loeb Classical Library, trans. F. C. Babbitt, Heinemann 1956: "A Letter to Apollonius", pp. 105–211.

6. Seneca, *Moral Essays* II, Loeb Classical Library, trans. J. W. Basore, Heinemann 1958: "de Consolatione ad Marciam", "de Consolatione ad Polybium", and "de Consolatione ad Helviam", Introd. p. ix.

7. *Moral Essays* II, op. cit.

8. Seneca, *Ad Lucilium Epistulae Morales*, Loeb Classical Library, trans. R. M. Gummere, Heinemann 1958: Letters LXIII and XCIX.

9. St Basil, *Letters*, Loeb Classical Library, trans. R. J. Deferrari, Heinemann 1926: Letters V, VI, CCLXIX, and CCCI.

10. *St Ambrose*, Library of Fathers of the Holy Catholic Church, James Parker, 1881. The possibility of our sadness affecting the happiness of the departed is expressed in Longfellow's *Hiawatha*.

> We are ghosts of the departed,
> Souls of those who once were with you.
> . . . Hither have we come to try you
> Hither have we come to warn you.
> Cries of grief and lamentation
> Reach us in the Blessed Islands;
> Cries of anguish from the living
> Calling back their friends departed,
> Sadden us with useless sorrow. . . .
> Think of this, O Hiawatha!
> Speak of it to all the people,
> That henceforward and for ever

> They no more with lamentations
> Sadden the souls of the departed. . . .

One of the Letters in *Dying We Live*, T. Huddleston (ed.), Fontana 1962, p. 177, ends with similar thoughts: "And—do not make it difficult for me 'over there' with tears."

11. St Jerome, *Select Letters*, Loeb Classical Library, trans. F. A. Wright, Heinemann 1954: Letter LX, p. 264ff.

12. *On the Decease of Satyrus*, Book I. 10.

13. *Smith's Dictionary of Christian Antiquity*, p. 253.

14. *Confessions*, IX.11.12.

15. Lowther Clarke (ed.), *Liturgy and Worship*, S.P.C.K. 1940: art. "The Burial of the Dead" by A. S. Duncan Jones, pp. 616–25.

16. See the Rubric: "When there is a special celebration . . .", and also the special Collect, Epistle, and Gospel appointed for All Souls Day, 2 November.

17. Modern critics might perhaps say that the 1662 Office is too gloomy and sombre. In his *Memorials*, Sir Edward Burne-Jones passes this comment on Browning's funeral: "I would have given something for a banner or two; and much would I have given if a chorister had come out of the triforium and rent the air with a trumpet." At the time of Sir Winston Churchill's death Mr Adlai Stevenson, United States Ambassador to the United Nations, said in the Memorial Service in Washington Cathedral, "We may be sad but we rejoice as well." See also *Alternative Services: Second Series*, The Church of England Liturgical Commission, S.P.C.K. 1966. "The Burial of the Dead", pp. 101–41.

18. Alix and George Reindorp, *Death and Those We Love*, Mothers' Union 1964.

19. cf. "Miserere—Gloria", epitaph to Henry Vaughan.

20. Raymond Raynes, c.r., *Darkness No Darkness*, Faith Press 1958, pp. 60–1.

CHAPTER 2

1. John Bowlby, "Grief and Mourning in Infancy", in *Psychoanalytic Study of the Child* 15, 1960, pp. 9–52.

2. A wonderful account in story form of how death can be explained to children is found in *Anne and the Sand Dobbies: A Story about Death for Children and their Parents*, John B. Coburn, Seabury Press 1964.

3. Joshua Liebman, *Peace of Mind*, Heinemann 1946, p. 129. Cf. Jean Guitton: "I remember when I was a child, daring to ask my mother what death was. She opened the Gospel of St John and

read: 'Jesus knowing that his hour was come, that he should pass out of this world to the Father; having loved his own who were in the world, he loved them unto the end. . . .' That is death, she said, to go to the Father, to love unto the end. After that, I asked no further questions."

4. Herman Feifel (ed.), *The Meaning of Death*, McGraw-Hill Book Co. 1959: "The Child's View of Death", by Maria H. Nagy, pp. 79–99.

5. Sylvia Anthony, *The Child's Discovery of Death*, Routledge and Kegan Paul 1940.

6. L. M. Chaloner, *Bereavement: To Lose One's Husband*, Delisle 1959, p. 9.

7. "An Experiment in Interpreting Death to Children", art. by Pauline Best in *The Journal of Pastoral Care*, Spring 1948.

8. Geoffrey Gorer, *Death, Grief and Mourning*, Cresset Press 1965, pp. 23–4.

9. Sylvia Anthony, op. cit.

10. F. Ilig and L. Armes, *Child Behaviour*, Dell Publishing Co., N.Y. 1955.

11. Marion Lanzer, *Learning to Live as a Widow*.

12. Margaret Torrie, *The Widow's Child*, Cruse Clubs 1964.

13. Ibid.

14. D. W. Winnicot, *The Child, the Family and the Outside World*, Pelican 1964, p. 115.

15. Cf. Margaret Wynn, *Fatherless Families*, Michael Joseph 1964: "We do not know enough about how to compensate a child for the loss of his father. The consequences of that loss and the effect on the child of being brought up without a father or father substitute have not been sufficiently studied. The effects of maternal deprivation on the other hand have been examined and re-examined . . . If a child loses his mother, attempts are made to replace her. If he loses his father, no such attempts are at present accepted as being at all necessary" (p. 13).

16. See further studies:

C. M. Parkes, "Recent Bereavement as a Cause of Mental Illness" in *British Journal of Psychiatry* Vol. 110, 1964, pp. 198–204.
C. M. Parkes, "Effects of Bereavement on Physical and Mental Health" in *British Medical Journal*, 1 August 1964, pp. 274f.
Hilgard, Newman, and Fisk, "Strength of Adult Ego following Childhood Bereavement" in *American Journal of Psychiatry*, No. 30, 1959, pp. 788–98.

Herbert Barry, "Significance of Maternal Bereavement before Age of Eight in Psychiatric Patients" in *Archives of Neurology and Psychiatry*, No. 62, 1949, pp. 630f.

17. "Depression and Childhood Bereavement", art. by Felix Brown in *Journal of Mental Science*, Vol. 107, p. 154. Sylvia Anthony (op. cit., p. 205) considers that the years eight to twelve are the most traumatic time for the loss of parents.

18. Joan Evelyn, *Widowhood*, Mowbray 1960, p. 43.

19. Margaret Torrie reminds us that "the young bachelor of thirty still carrying his mother's shopping basket and accompanying her everywhere, can be emotionally handicapped. Waiting on a boy hand and foot has its dangers too. One such lad of sixteen became extremely aggressive and disturbed when his widowed mother began to turn her attentions to a would-be suitor. He had thought he was the master of the house and when the mother married the suitor there was major trouble. Sons need male company, boy friends and clubs to counter the unavoidable petticoat government in the widow's home. They should never be encouraged to become 'substitute husbands'" (op. cit., p. 8).

20. Joan Evelyn, op. cit., p. 44.

21. See Pension Lists, pp. 189ff above.

22. "Loneliness", art. by Professor John Cohen in *Family Doctor*, December 1964.

23. P. Sainsbury (*Suicides in London*, 1958, p. 81) reports that suicides are more common among the widowed than among the single. See also Peter Townsend, *The Family Life of Old People*, Pelican 1963: Chapter 13: "Isolation, Loneliness, and Hold on Life", pp. 188–205.

24. "Help in Time of Sorrow", art. in *Readers' Digest*, January 1964, pp. 124–6 (italics my own).

CHAPTER 3

1. Peter Marris, *Widows and their Families*, Routledge and Kegan Paul 1958. Foreword by Dr John Bowlby, p. ix.

2. *Collected Papers*, The International Psychoanalytical Library, Hogarth Press 1948, Vol. IV, pp. 152–70.

3. In *American Journal of Psychiatry*, Vol. 101, No. 2, September 1944.

4. Further recent studies on bereavement have been carried out by:
   K. Stern, G. W. Williams, and M. Prados, "Grief Reactions in later life" in *American Journal of Psychiatry*, No. 108, October 1951, pp. 289f.
   C. E. Benda, "Bereavement and Grief Work", paper given in University of Buffalo School of Medicine, 18 October 1961.

J. Bowlby, "Grief and Mourning in Infancy" in *Psychoanalytic Study of the Child*, International University Press, N.Y. 1961, p. 15.

C. M. Parkes, "Effects of Bereavement on Physical and Mental Health" in *British Medical Journal*, 1 August 1964, pp. 274f.

C. M. Parkes, "Grief as an Illness" in *New Society*, 9 April 1964.

5. C. S. Lewis, *A Grief Observed*, Faber and Faber 1961.

6. "Grief Must be Faced" in *The Christian Century*, 28 February 1945, p. 269. Quoted by Paul Irion, *The Funeral and the Mourners*, Abingdon Press 1954, p. 52.

7. *Widows and their Families*, p. 25.

8. Anne Philipe, *No longer than a Sigh*, Michael Joseph 1964, p. 29.

9. See "Grief Reactions in Later Life", by K. Stern and others, in *American Journal of Psychiatry* 108, 1951, pp. 289–94.

10. E. Weiss, *Principles of Psychodynamics*, pp. 10–11. Quoted in "Understanding Grief", Edgar N. Jackson, Abingdon Press 1957, p. 147.

11. *Widows and their Families*, p. 15.

12. *Widowhood*, p. 22.

13. *Confessions*, IV.

14. Linn and Schwarz, *Psychiatry and Religious Experience*, Random House 1958, p. 179.

15. For further reading see:
    Young and Meiburg, *Spiritual Therapy*, Hodder and Stoughton 1961, chapter III.

    H. H. Brewster, "Separation Reaction in Psychosomatic Disease and Neurosis", in *Psychosomatic Medicine*, No. 3, 1952, pp. 154f.

    V. M. Nagler, *Emotional Problems of Cancer Patients*, Kershaw Press 1961.

16. See E. Durkheim, *Suicide*, London 1952, p. 259: "The suicides occurring at the crisis of widowhood . . . are really due to domestic anomaly resulting from the death of husband or wife. A family catastrophe occurs which affects the survivor. He is not adapted to the new situation in which he finds himself and accordingly offers less resistance to suicide."

17. "Effects of Bereavement on Physical and Mental Health: A Study of the Medical Record of Widows" in *British Medical Journal*, 1 August 1964, pp. 274f.

18. C. M. Parkes, "Grief as an Illness", in *New Society*, April 1964, p. 12.

CHAPTER 4

1. Emile Cammaerts, *Upon This Rock*, Cresset Press 1942, p. 98.

2. E. B. Browning, "Grief".

3. In James Agee's *A Death in the Family* (Avon Book, 11th Printing, 1963, pp. 127–8), Aunt Hannah comforts Mary, whose husband has been killed in an accident, by helping her to express her grief. She "stooped before Mary, taking her wrists and talking earnestly into her streaming hands: 'Mary, listen to me, Mary. There's nothing to ask forgiveness for . . . Do you hear me, Mary?' Mary nodded within her hands. 'God would never ask of you not to grieve, not to cry. Do you hear? What you're doing is absolutely natural, absolutely right. Do you hear? You wouldn't be human if you did otherwise . . .'."

4. Joshua Loth Liebman, *Peace of Mind*, Heinemann 1946, p. 125.

5. *Venture to the Interior*, Penguin 1963, p. 144.

6. *The Lamps still Burn*, Cornish Bros. 1945.

7. *Upon This Rock*, pp. 81–2.

8. See Gorer, *Death, Grief and Mourning*, pp. 72f, for further patterns of mourning observed by the Orthodox Jews.

9. *Peace of Mind*, p. 123 (italics my own).

10. "Needs of the Bereaved", art. by William F. Rogers in *Bereavemen—Death—The Funeral*, edited by Simon Doninger, Pastoral Psychology Press, 1955.

11. Ibid., p. 22.

12. Edgar N. Jackson, *Understanding Grief*, Abingdon Press 1957, pp. 180–1.

13. Gerald Caplan, *An Approach to Community Mental Health*, Tavistock Publ. 1961, pp. 218–22.

14. Paul Gliddon and Muriel Powell, *Called to Serve*, Hodder and Stoughton 1952, p. 121.

15. Peter Marris, *Widows and their Families*, Routledge and Kegan Paul 1958, p. 125.

16. Charles Bachmann, *Ministering to the Grief Sufferer*, Prentice-Hall Inc. 1964, p. 33.

17. *Pastoral Theology*, Edinburgh 1855, trans. from French.

18. "Bereavement and Grief Work", by Clemens E. Benda, paper given at University of Buffalo School of Medicine, 18 October 1961.

19. "Grief as an Illness", C. Murray Parkes in *New Society*, 9 April 1964.

20. See "Funeral Director" section, p. 93 above.

CHAPTER 5

1. *A Grief Observed*, p. 43.

2. Edward T. Vernon, *Where Grave Thy Victory?* St Andrew Press 1955. Cf. Wm Wand, *Changeful Page*, Hodder & Stoughton 1965, p. 129: "I tremble to think what must be the agony of those who have no hope of seeing their dear ones again. To us half the meaning of life is now made up of his immediate presence and the future union." Bishop Wand's son, Paul, was killed climbing in the Alps.

3. E. E. Holmes, *Immortality*, Longmans 1908, pp. 137–8.

4. Cf. John Betjeman's lines in "House of Rest" about an aged widow of a clergyman, living alone, when "all the world is dead":

> Now when the bells for Eucharist
> Sound in the Market Square,
> With sunshine struggling through the mist,
> And Sunday in the air,
>
> The veil between her and her dead
> Dissolves and shows them clear,
> The Consecration Prayer is said,
> And all of them are near.

5. W. R. Inge, *Personal Religion and the life of Devotion*, Longmans 1924, pp. 88–9.

Part Two

1 The Cremation Regulations 1965: S.I. 1146, H.M.S.O. [6a] simplify procedures for cremation. A householder to whom the applicant is known can now countersign the application for cremation instead of a member of certain classes of persons such as ministers of religion or solicitors. Roman Catholics are now permitted to arrange cremations by the Papal Decree of 1963.

2 The Church Information Office, Church House, Westminster, S.W.1 publishes a most useful pamphlet on *The Disposal of Cremated Remains*, April 1965. Price 9d. or 25s. per 50 copies.

Other helpful literature:

(a) *The Care of Churchyards*, C.I.O., 4th edn, 1952.
(b) *Advice Concerning Cremation as part of Christian Burial*, S.P.C.K. Pamphlets. Approved by Archbishops of Canterbury and York.
(c) *Closed Churchyards*, Legal Board of Church Assembly Leaflet.
(d) *Arranging a Funeral*, distributed through Citizens' Advice Bureaux, Consumer Council, 3 Cornwall Terrace, N.W.1.

Index of Subjects

Index of
Proper Names, Authors, Books
and Journals